When Answers Aren't Enough

Matt Rogers

When Answers Aren't Enough

Experiencing God as Good
When Life Isn't

ZONDERVAN®

ZONDERVAN.com/
AUTHORTRACKER
follow your favorite authors

When Answers Aren't Enough
Copyright © 2008 by Matt Rogers

Requests for information should be addressed to:
Zondervan, *Grand Rapids, Michigan 49530*

Library of Congress Cataloging-in-Publication Data

Rogers, Matt, 1977 –
    When answers aren't enough : experiencing God as good when life isn't /
Matt Rogers.
      p. cm.
    ISBN 978-0-310-28681-3 (softcover)
    1. God (Christianity) – Goodness. 2. Consolation. 3. Virginia Tech Shootings,
Blacksburg, Va., 2007. I. Title.
    BT137.R64   2008
    231'.8 – dc22   2008002730

Published in assciation with the literary agency of Daniel Literary Group, LLC, 1701 Kingsbury Drive, Suite 100, Nashville, TN 37215.

Some details have been changed in order to protect the privacy of individuals whose stories are told here.

Interior design by Beth Shagene
Printed in the United States of America

08 09 10 11 12 13 14 • 23 22 21 20 19 18 17 16 15 14 13 12 11 10 9 8 7 6 5 4 3 2 1

To Madeleine L'Engle
for showing me something better than intellect alone;
for teaching me to experience what I once only believed.

———

About the Book

Likely, the title has given it away: this is not a book of answers. If you are seeking possible solutions to the troubling questions that arise in times of suffering, may I suggest Philip Yancey's works *Where Is God When It Hurts?* and *Disappointment with God.* I know of no better books on the problem of pain.

The book you now hold is a series of meditations, reflections on tragedy and on how we might experience God as good when answers fail to satisfy. You might think of what I've written as a private journal made public or as a letter from a friend.

From the beginning, I decided to write this book as a story, a personal journey, since this is, in fact, how life comes to each of us. Much of it is written in the present tense, as though it were happening now, so that you may join me on the road. Along the way, you may find at times that you disagree with something I've said. By all means, object. I welcome the interaction as we travel together.

In writing this book, one problem quickly arose with my approach to telling a story. What should I do with a conversation I had during the timeline of part 3 of the book when the content of that conversation fit more naturally in part 1? If I insisted on a perfectly linear telling of events, the book would state in one part what it had already said in an earlier part, and that would frustrate the reader: *Why does the author keep repeating himself?* At times, therefore, I have moved a story here or there to ensure a more acceptable pace to the book. The stories are, however, all true (if at times anachronistic).

Part 1 begins soon after the shootings at Virginia Tech and is, for that reason, the rawest and roughest around the edges. I have intentionally kept the early pages grim; too many Christian books skip too quickly to hope, leaping over thoughts and feelings germane to people in pain. The result is a work that may be true but doesn't sound real. My goal is to see how we might experience God as good when we are covered in sadness. To do so, things must seem truly bad before they can get better.

Part 2 is a call to remember the world as it was before grief and suffering marred it. If there is a good creation buried beneath the brokenness, then perhaps there is a good God who designed it. Can we find him? Can we taste and see that he is good?

Part 3 is the "Where to from here?" It seeks to imagine the world that will be when God's will on earth is done as it is in heaven. Consequently, and not surprisingly, this is the most hopeful portion of the book—though I think you'll find a good deal of joy throughout.

From start to finish, I have written with author Annie Dillard's exhortation in mind:

> Write as if you were dying. At the same time, assume you write for an audience consisting solely of terminal patients. That is, after all, the case. What would you begin writing if you knew

you would die soon? What could you say to a dying person that would not enrage by its triviality?[1]

Here is my attempt at answering Dillard's questions. Here is my journey. I hope you'll walk with me on the way.

Matt

Preface

I was waking up, lured out of sleep by a low and distant rumble and thud. My hazy, slumbering mind at first dismissed the sound as road construction, echoing up from the street outside my window. I rolled over, tried to ignore it, but it came closer, grew louder. As my mind surfaced from sleep, I picked up the perfectly timed repetition. *Rumble and thud*. Pause. *Rumble and thud*. Pause. *Rumble and thud*.

Had to be a drum. I pulled myself from under the covers and, rising, shuffled groggily to the window to open the blinds. Eyes adjusting to the light, I saw a seemingly endless stream of blue-and-white-clad cadets marching slowly, somberly, one after the other, into the cemetery across the street from my house. It looked like an invasion. But the stoic faces gave it away. I knew immediately what this must be.

A few days earlier, on the evening of April 16, 2007, Chris Hutto, a home group leader in the church I copastor at Virginia Tech, clung anxiously to a cell phone, waiting for word, for good news, about his friend Matt La Porte. All anyone knew was that thirty-three students and faculty were dead, and an undetermined number of others injured, in the worst mass shooting in modern U.S. history. Something was certainly wrong with Matt—he would have called by now—but perhaps he was only injured. Chris nervously fiddled and fumbled and held to the phone for good news that would never come. Matthew Joseph La Porte, just twenty years old, was gone.

The first days following the shootings were a blur. I got up early and stayed up late, talking with students, answering reporters' questions, and helping in whatever little ways I could. The days were exhaustingly long. I finally found a few minutes one afternoon to rest and lay down for a quick nap. I was out immediately. Only minutes later came the rumble and thud of that solemn drumbeat, dragging me back to the wakened world I wanted so badly to escape. *I cannot even hide from this in sleep.*

I was clinging, holding on, like Chris to his cell phone, to the dream that maybe life wasn't all that bad. But as I stood at the window, waking up, peering through the blinds and watching the mournful march, a heavy, sinking sadness set in. I thought of Matt La Porte the previous Monday, dressed in his Corps uniform, on his way to class in Norris Hall—Was he running late? Did he hurry to get there?—absolutely unaware. Unaware that he was breathing in his last crisp mountain air; feeling a final blast of Blacksburg wind; watching snowflakes flitter and fall, out of season—the last of a lingering winter, and the last of Matt's short life.

I watched from the window as long as I could. The entire Virginia Tech Corps of Cadets, some seven hundred strong, marched into the cemetery, up over a hill, and out of sight to say good-bye to Matt.

I was still waking up.

—

It was not the Virginia Tech shootings alone that set me on my jour-ney this summer. I received a call late one night, nearly a month af-terward. The caller ID on my cell phone read "Mom and Dad." I knew instantly that something was wrong. They were usually in bed by ten o'clock, and it was almost midnight. I answered the phone, and a shaken voice answered back.

"Matt, it's Mom."

My face flushed, and my heart began racing as I waited to hear what had happened.

"I'm at the hospital with your dad. He fell off the roof cleaning gutters tonight." Interrupting herself, and sounding as if she were try-ing to convince herself more than me, Mom interjected, "He's okay though. He has a broken arm and his face is pretty banged up — his jaw is broken — but he's awake."

"Are *you* okay?" I asked.

There was a long pause, and then a wavering response. "Yes," Mom said, obviously crying. "I'm fine. I didn't want to call, but your dad keeps saying he wants you to come home."

I held back the fear of the "what if" questions long enough to pack. What if he *wasn't* okay? What if he wasn't going to be okay? *You can think about that in the car.* I threw a few shirts and some jeans in a bag. *How long will I be there? Do I need a suit? Am I going to a funeral?*

It's the waiting that is hard, waiting to learn the fate of a loved one, like Chris had waited in vain for good news about his friend Matt. I waited for three hours on the drive down to North Carolina, wondering whether Mom had been totally truthful about Dad's con-dition. Dad had fallen off the roof that evening at seven, but no one called until midnight. Had things taken a turn for the worse? Why was Dad asking for me to come?

The situation was, more or less, as Mom had described when I arrived at the hospital in Charlotte. Dad was awake and talking, though mostly nonsensically due to heavy medication and the trauma of the impact. He had landed face-first on the wooden deck behind the house, bracing himself only slightly with his left arm, now broken in several spots. His head on one side was swollen to what seemed twice its size, and a steady trickle of blood ran from his right ear, staining the starchy white pillow beneath.

The sight sickened me. I am not usually bothered by blood or needles or hospitals, but the image of my dad, mumbling through a fractured jaw, grimacing now and then in pain, was nauseating. I tried to lighten the mood: "Took a little fall, did we?" I said, smiling to hide the shock of seeing Dad broken for the first time in my life.

Over the next couple of days, Dad drifted in and out of lucidity. At moments, he was hysterically funny from morphine; at others, he was vulgar and crass. He couldn't help any of it, of course; he couldn't choose his demeanor. The drugs did that for him. The hours when he was especially distant and foggy, I had the awful sense that I was glimpsing the future when my parents would be old. And it was as if, in his drug-induced state, my dad somehow knew this. He seemed to read my thoughts, and lacking any filter for his own, he said with a wry smile, "This is just the start of what you have to look forward to, Son, the older your mom and I get."

I had to leave the room. Strange how, at age thirty, in an instant of blinding clarity, I could learn what I had known all my life. That my parents are not immune to death was obvious, but I do not believe I had ever come so close to imagining what that inevitable day might be like as I did standing over my father's hospital bed, watching him come and go from reality. For all its high tragedy, its terrible death toll, its dizzying media blitz, and its sweetly somber vigils, April 16 was unable to do what this one simple moment did in bringing my childish hopes down around me. *We will not avoid finality. None of us will. Not even . . .*

My dad is fifty-eight. Average life expectancy in the United States is about seventy-eight years. *If my dad is average . . .* I began to do the math. *Twenty Christmases left, if we're lucky.* Reality came sharply, screamingly into focus, as if for three decades I'd lived under anesthesia and was just waking up and coming to, finding out what the real world was all about. What thirty-three families found out a month ago. What we all must eventually find out, whether death comes by tragedy or simply by old age. Suddenly I hated hospitals, everything about them, what they represented, that people are (that my dad is) temporary, finite, leaving. I have never been naive, so the eventuality of death did not catch me by surprise. What stunned me that day, in words from a father drugged out of his mind, was how fast the end was gaining on us.

I tried for two days to lull myself back to sleep, back under the anesthesia, but I was wide awake now. Dad came through surgery on his arm fine, and afterward, as soon as I could, I got on the road, got away, and headed home to Virginia. I felt guilty for leaving so soon, Dad still recovering, but everyone acknowledged there was nothing more for me to do, that I had a job to get back to. Much of the way home, I was like a man holding his breath, badly needing to exhale, to let it all out.

Just before the Virginia border, I passed a patch of brightly colored wildflowers dancing in the breeze, showing off their brilliant shades of red, purple, and gold. After a week of nothing beautiful, of days spent staring at the off-white sterility of hospital walls and hallways, flowers looked out of place in the world, as if they all should have died with that phone call from Mom at midnight.

As the flowers flew by in a blur and then faded from sight in my rearview mirror, I wondered, How can this world be, in the same instant, so beautiful and yet so awful? I thought of what Jesus said one day on a hillside, how if God clothes the lilies so extravagantly, how much more will he care for us? "Look at the birds of the air," he said. "They do not sow or reap or store away in barns, and yet your heavenly Father feeds them. Are you not much more valuable than they?"[1] *One would have thought.*

"Not a single sparrow can fall to the ground without your Father knowing it."[2] *Really? What about my dad? What about Matt La Porte? Or the thirty-two others? Or the two hundred Iraqis who died the same day but barely got a mention in the news because the focus was on my school? Or how about the six million Jews who fell to the ground in the Holocaust? Did the Father see them?*

Tears blurred the road in front of me as the pressure in my chest built toward eruption. The grief of the past week — of the past month — had finally come calling, rising up, until at last I slammed my fist on the steering wheel, looked toward heaven, and exploded. "God, I am not okay with this! I'm not okay with this world! I'm not okay with death, with my dad's mortality! I cannot understand how you can let this world go on and on and on like it is, year after year. I know you are good. I know none of this is your fault. But knowing that doesn't make it any better. I'm not okay with this, God."

—

I'm still not.

I do believe God is good. Remember, I'm a pastor. I affirmed that belief to my congregation after the April 16 shootings. I affirm it now. And I know how to work out in my head the familiar "why" questions people ask after tragedy.

If God is good, why is there so much suffering in the world? It's simple, really. One doesn't need even a paragraph to explain it; a couple of sentences will do. God made people to walk in love toward him and toward each other. Man rebelled against God, walked away from that most essential of relationships, and the result has been the suffering and evil and war and death that we see every day.

Why doesn't God just stop it? Again, simple. Scripture says God made humans in his image. Whatever else that means, it at least means we, like God, have a will, the ability to choose our actions. We can choose to love goodness or to love evil. Some people sadly opt for evil, and the result is suffering. But if God ever took from us that choice, he would be taking from us his image. We would be animals, not humans.

See, I know the answers. I know them by heart and can even recite them in my sleep. But what I've learned this spring is that sometimes answers aren't enough. They can carry us far, but only so far. Then what? When we can answer our own questions but our hearts still ache, then what? When we can outwit and outdebate every atheist objection to the reality and goodness of God, yet our dad still lays bruised, bloodied, and broken—then what?

We've dodged a bullet with Dad. The doctors say he will be fine. He'll need more surgery and then therapy for his arm, but his jaw should heal on its own. And once he is off the pain medication, his normal demeanor will return. It could have been a lot worse.

It will be one day. Dad will not dodge the bullet of death forever, as thirty-three others did not this spring. Nor will I dodge the bullet of dealing with his death. Then what?

I believe God is good, but how do I *experience* him as good when life isn't? There must be a way. The psalmist says, "Taste and see that the LORD is good."[3] "Go beyond the intellect, beyond mere knowledge," he says. "Taste it. See it. *Experience* it!" But how can I when the world is dark and grief is raining down?

Spring this year has been a season of waking up, of coming to see the world as it truly is, the blinders off. And I do not want to run any longer from what I've found, despite the horror and sadness and the innocence lost. I do not want to hide from it, not even for a second. To hide is to live a lie, a fantasy. Ours is a real world, and I want to find a way of embracing it, as Jesus did. I want to remember what it was he intended for this world, his original dream, for surely what I've seen this spring is not it. And I want to live as he did—joyfully, expectantly—as if that dream were still a possibility.

Jesus lived fully aware of the darkness yet not overcome by it at all. I am not sure yet how one does that, but I want to find a way. (Again, there has to be a way.) But I know simple answers will not—*cannot*—get me there. Peace lies along a different path, and so I begin a journey to find it.

This will be a time of discovery.

Part 1

A Heavy, Sinking Sadness

Embracing the World That Is

One

Lately I've been walking in the evenings. I tend to do that when stuck on a question. Maybe I'm trying to walk it off. On days when I have time, I drive out to Pandapas Pond in Jefferson National Forest to be in nature. Once there, I set off through the woods or slowly stroll along the water's edge, deep in thought or prayer.

Most days, because of time, I have to settle for the streets around my home. I can quickly climb to the top of Lee Street, turn around, and look out over Blacksburg, the Blue Ridge backlit by the setting sun. From there, I can see much of Virginia Tech. The stately bell tower of Burruss Hall rises proudly above the rest.

On nights like tonight, when I get a late start and the sun is already down, I head for campus. At its center, separating the academic and residential sides of the school, sits the Drill Field, a wide-open grassy space named for the exercises that the Corps of Cadets practices to perfection there. After dark, old iron lampposts, painted black, blanket the ground in overlapping circles of light.

It was here on the Drill Field, the day after the shootings, that students placed thirty-two slabs of gray limestone rock — Hokie stones, as they're called — in a semicircle in front of Burruss Hall, to commemorate the lives of loved ones lost. Thousands of mourners descended on the place, bearing with them a flood of condolences, a mix of bouquets, balloons, and poster-board sympathies. They came sniffling, clinging to tissues and to one another, and lifting their sunglasses to wipe tears from their tired, red eyes. The world came as well, vicariously through television, watching us, kneeling with us in grief.

I also came, revisiting the stones day after day, and sometimes at night, drawn to them by a need to connect with the dead whom I never knew. Always there was something new here, some trinket that had been added. At times the items seemed odd: a baseball for every victim, an American flag by every stone, though some of the dead were international students.

People took their time passing by this spot. There was no need to rush; there were no classes to attend. It would be days, dark and long, before there would be any distractions from the pain. For a time, there was no world beyond this place.

By day, soft chatter could be heard around the memorial. After sunset, no one spoke a word. During daylight, masses huddled near the stones, peering over shoulders to read the notes left there. At night, however, mourners passed by in a single-file line, waiting their turn, patient with the people in front who wished to pause at every name.

The masses have since receded. The Drill Field now is vacant (except for these stones) and silent. The semester has ended, most of the students are gone, and only the sounds of insects disturb the stillness of the summer evening air. If I close my eyes and take in the quiet, I can almost imagine nothing happened here.

Almost. Except for the stone reminders that lie at my feet. On one is written a simple, anguished note.

> Jeremy,
> We love you.
> Mom and Dad

These stones are more than rocks. Each is all that remains of a son, a daughter, a husband who will never come home again. I picture my mom and dad, heartbroken, kneeling by a stone for me, had I been among the dead. Moreover, I imagine myself by a stone for my dad, had he not survived his fall.

This is a summer of mourning. I am grieving the world as it is. And I am asking, "If I embrace the world as it is, in all its sadness—if I refuse to bury my head in the sand, pretending all is well, but rather think and speak of the world as it actually is—can I, then, still know God as good? Can my experience of him be more consistent than my circumstances, which alternate between good and bad?"

Is this too much to expect?

Before I can know, I must face the world at its worst.

Two

The apostle Paul, in a fit of rapture, wrote, "Where, O death, is your sting?"[1] I feel like firing back, "Where, O Paul, *isn't* it?" Death is all around me this summer. It hangs over Blacksburg like a heavy cloud, as though it might rain down on us again.

Somewhere in the cemetery across from my home lies a young man named Matt. His only sin, that cold day in April, was getting up and going to class. For that, he's sealed in a coffin underground.

My next-door neighbor Faith told me this evening of her sister's death last week. Lung cancer, I believe she said.

My friend David just lost his dad unexpectedly.

And I cannot stop imagining how that call from Mom might have ended: "Matt, I'm at the hospital. Your dad passed away this evening."

Who's next?

And where? Aside from the headline-grabbing nature of the tragedy here, our story is that of any town, any corner of creation. *Find one place on this earth, O Paul, where death doesn't sting.*

I speak with students who, though they were nowhere near Norris Hall, have nightmares of what went on in there that day. Some are battling depression: "Will I ever be happy again?" Others fear: "Will there be copycat shootings?" I myself jump every time a firework goes off at the college apartment complex down the street. When a siren sounds, I wonder, *What now?* We will feel the sting of death here for some time.

I, like many others, no doubt, have felt it all my life.

My first real experience with death came when my baby brother, Michael Preston, was born prematurely and died a day old. I was just three at the time. Forever seared upon my mind is the memory of that moment my dad called my older brother, Brian, and me into the living room and gave us the news. I vividly recall falling into Dad's lap, burying my face in his shoulder, my arms wrapped around his neck, and squalling as only a confused and saddened three-year-old can.

Mostly I was crying for myself: for nine long months — *terribly* long to a young child squirming with anticipation — Mom had told me I was going to have a brother. My very own brother! I had not yet mastered the family tree concept, didn't understand that Preston would also be my older brother's brother. No, he was mine! Mine alone. And like a kid holding out for Christmas morning, I dreamed of playing with my new "toy."

Santa never came. Worse: he came but took back his toy. Though I've tried, I cannot recall the exact words Dad used to tell Brian and me that Preston wasn't coming home. Did he use the word we so often avoid, for which we substitute any number of euphemisms? Did he say Preston had "died"? All I remember — and I remember as if it happened last week — is falling on Dad in sudden, heavy grief.

Having never met my baby brother, I missed him anyway. To my great-aunt Geraldine, I said sadly, "Preston's gone up to heaven, and

A Heavy, Sinking Sadness

I can't even fly." However little I may have understood then about death, I grasped its permanence. Something precious, irreplaceable, was gone forever.

I have that feeling again this summer, as though I could cry for a brother I never knew. Many times after April 16, I gazed out my bedroom window, staring past trees still barren from winter, wondering how far over the hill in the distance lay Matt La Porte. And wondering why I felt the need to go looking for him.

The trees are dressed for summer now; I can no longer see the cemetery. But it's there, always in the back of my mind, as is the feeling that I should find Matt. He is a neighbor of sorts now, and tonight, as the sun begins to set, the compulsion to visit him overtakes me.

Josiah, a student in the Corps of Cadets, told me where exactly to find Matt, should I ever want to, but I've looked all over this place tonight, and I don't see him. Maybe the whole thing has been a bad dream. Maybe I'm finally waking up from April. When I'm almost ready to leave, it occurs that I've been searching for a permanent headstone. Matt has been here barely a month. There might be only a small marker, placed by the funeral home.

I wish cemeteries didn't pack people in so. I have to step on others' graves in search of Matt. I cannot step over them or around them, there are so many. Doesn't feel right. Next to Crystal, and one up from David, is a plot with freshly potted flowers over top but no stone. The ground over this grave is raised from the sod having not yet settled, and a thin bald strip of earth outlines the plot in the shape and size of a coffin; along these edges, the grass is struggling against a dry summer, fighting to live again after the upheaval. This is a new grave.

Something blue rests beside the flowerpot, a toy airplane. More specifically, a military jet. Was Matt going to be a pilot? Moving in, I see a small copper-colored rectangle at the head of the grave, a name and date inscribed thereon:

Matthew J. La Porte
1986 – 2007

I go to my knees, brought down by that sudden, heavy grief I remember well. Why am I here instead of Matt? Why have I been granted more life than was given to him?

I want to call down to him, to tell him how sorry I am. *I'm so sorry this happened to you.* And that I'm going to learn all I can from this so that he will not have died in vain. This need to talk with Matt is so strong, actual words slip out: "I'm sorry, Matt."

He is near, yet out of reach. So close and yet eternity stands between us. Just a few feet beneath me rests a man who, little more than a month ago, was bursting with young life, laughing with friends, planning for his future. Now he and his future have gone cold, distant, untouchable.

Kneeling here, I think of all the joys he'll never know. He'll never graduate or fly that plane. He'll never marry or celebrate the birth of his kids or his grandkids. I think of all the little things that made Matt unique, the slightest idiosyncrasies that distinguished him from any other Matt — any other being at all — in the world.

I wonder what simple pleasures made him smile. Chris Hutto, Matt's friend and fellow cadet, tells me how they used to meet for lunch — grilled cheese sandwiches at Schultz dining hall on campus. Earlier this year, on April 4, Chris wrote on Matt's online Facebook wall: "We should do lunch or dinner sometime again." Twelve days later, there was no more "sometime." No more "again."

I do not know whether Chris and Matt shared a final grilled cheese together, and I cannot bring myself to ask. But it is this little fact, that Matt loved grilled cheese, that brings me to the edge of tears. And it is for this reason I am drawn to Matt's graveside.

I need to see that Matt was more than a name on a victims list, more than a number in a death toll. He was a real man, with virtues and vices, like any of the rest of us. He has a real grave now, and real people, his friends and family, scrape to find a way through life without the Matt they loved so much.

How, O Paul, could this ever *not* sting?

Three

I once thought a good goal in life was getting over death. I thought I was supposed to. More than once I've heard, *Everybody dies. It's no big deal; don't worry about it.* Why, then, am I so haunted by death?

The first funeral I attended was for a neighbor across the street. She died in her sleep. I was maybe ten, plenty old enough, my parents thought, for a funeral.

Never will I forget seeing the body — ashen in tone, expressionless, and cold. I spent the whole service on the verge of vomiting. For weeks after, I could not watch a graveside scene in a film or television show.

Years later, after a best friend, Baker Falls, died, a man at the viewing exuberantly declared how much better off Baker was now that he was with God. No more leukemia. No more chemo. No more hair falling out or throwing up or IVs in the arm. No more hospital food. No more pain. On and on he went. *Enough! I get it. He's in heaven.*

He was still dead. Why was this other guy so thrilled at the thought of where Baker was, when all I could think was how much I wished he were here with us? Adding to the pain were all the people who told me repeatedly in the days that followed, "Life goes on!"

In a sense, that statement was true — life did go on. I still went to work, still ate meals as before. I took my shower every morning as if all were normal. I fulfilled my responsibilities to my church, same as I otherwise would have. Life went on, but it did not go on the same as before. What a terribly flippant thing to say: "Life goes on!" You might say such a thing when you've been turned down for a job or when you have a flat tire. Not when a best friend dies.

People say ridiculous things when speaking of death. "Life goes on." "It was his time." "Death is natural, just a part of life." Where did we learn this? Am I the only one who thinks death is the most unnatural thing in the universe?

At Baker's viewing, I remember not seeing him at first, only the casket. Then a bit of the padding came into view. Then my friend. His face appeared very gray, almost metallic, not Baker's usual warm, soft complexion. And his body was swollen, presumably from the steroids doctors gave him. His head was bald, a reminder of his chemotherapy.

This wasn't Baker. I had seen him with no hair, but the skin was wrong. His weight was wrong. And the absent smile was wrong. This looked more like a wax figure than the friend I had embraced so many times.

After moving through the line, past the family to offer condolences, I sat down on a pew in the hallway, facing into the room. Facing Baker's casket. He looked a little more natural from a distance.

Death always appears more natural from a distance. Is this why we keep it at arm's length, view it from across the room? Ignore it or try to get okay with it?

"Death is just a part of life." Could any statement be more absurd, more nonsensical? I cringe when people say it. Death and life are opposites. Neither can take part in the other. We know this. What, then, makes us say such silly, syrupy things? "Death is natural." Is this our way of getting over, getting okay with, the indescribably awful? We know we can't beat it, so why not make peace with it, pretend it isn't, after all, that bad. That is something we must never do.

I recently saw a film that was a simple tale of life, then death. The woman in the story, freshly bereaved, poured out the ashes of her husband in a ceremony by a river. Most of the "body" fell to the ground in an undignified clump. The rest scattered on the breeze, fluttered over the water, and fell in, carried downstream by the current.

I nearly threw up. *You just spilled your husband on the ground!* I thought. *How can we sit here in a theater watching this, unmoved?* I cannot believe I am the only one bothered to my core by all this. If I did believe I was the only one, I'd never share my journey. I'd keep it to myself, locked away in a journal somewhere. But there must be others who feel this way.

I have a friend who tells me he's unbothered by death. I don't mean that he is unafraid, just that death doesn't matter to him. It's just how it is, how life ends. Everybody dies. No big deal.

How can this be? How can we stand to bury beloved flesh? How can we say good-bye to those with whom we've laughed and danced and made love? The body is central to our faith, though we often speak as if it were only our soul that matters. Those who denied Jesus had come in flesh were rightly denounced as heretics. How, then, can we help but mourn decay? How could we ever dump out our loved ones in a clump of ash and not throw up?

Every funeral I see is one more reminder that something has gone horribly wrong in the universe. Every cemetery is a scar on the skin of creation; every grave, an ugly gash that was never meant to be. At the deepest level of my being, I know this is not how the world was supposed to be.

Do we not all long for eternity? Has not God, as the ecclesiastical writer said, "set eternity in the human heart"?[2] Should not our souls, then, scream at the thought of death? "But it was his time; he lived a full life." No! It's *never* someone's time. No life is as full as it might have been, as it *should* have been.

Have we forgotten the curse that followed our fall? "For dust you are and to dust you will return."[3] It's a curse! Not something natural (at least not as nature was intended), not something with which to make peace. If the goal of God is to restore creation, to redeem it, how can we raise the white flag and give in to that which has marred the earth?

We are so quick to jump to the apostle Paul's statement that "to live is Christ and to die is gain."[4] But it's worth noting that whatever pleasure Paul received in death, in being reunited with Christ, his comment was not a peace treaty with mortality. The same Paul who said that death is gain also said that "the last enemy to be destroyed is death."[5]

Death is a villain, a particularly insidious one. It is a cancer on the earth, tenacious and spreading. God means to destroy it one day. Until then, we bury Matt La Porte, and my neighbor's sister, and my friend David's dad, and my friend Baker.

God forgive us if we ever get okay with that.

I cannot embrace the curse, but I must find a way of embracing this world, of living in a marred creation that, for now, permits death. And I must find a way of experiencing God as good in the midst of the awful dust and ash.

Four

I've begun reading *Night*, Elie Wiesel's memoir of the Holocaust. (My friend John tells me, "Dude, you need some cartoons.") Wiesel escaped Hitler's death camps with his life, but not with his family (who died before the liberators came) or his faith.

> Never shall I forget that night, the first night in camp, that
> turned my life into one long night seven times sealed.
> Never shall I forget that smoke.
> Never shall I forget the small faces of the children whose bodies
> I saw transformed into smoke under a silent sky.
> Never shall I forget those flames that consumed my faith forever.
> Never shall I forget the nocturnal silence that deprived me for all
> eternity of the desire to live.
> Never shall I forget those moments that murdered my God and
> my soul and turned my dreams to ashes.
> Never shall I forget those things, even were I condemned to live
> as long as God Himself.
> Never.[6]

Confronted with a darkness so terrifying he could only name it Night, Wiesel lost his confidence in, and certainly the experience of, any goodness in God. "Why should I sanctify His name?" Wiesel asked. "The Almighty, the eternal and terrible Master of the Universe, chose to be silent. What was there to thank Him for?"[7]

Would this be my response as well? Would we all say the same if faced with similar evil?

Elie Wiesel was a teenager when he was taken by the Nazis, not much younger than those injured or killed on April 16. What would the survivors of this most recent tragedy say? Could I find one among them who would still confess, "I've tasted and I've seen: God is good, even when life isn't"? And could he show me how to experience this for myself, when the bottom of my life falls out?

───

Hands cold and clammy, I knock, step back, and wait nervously for what seems an eternity for the door to open. From inside the apartment, I can hear footsteps moving closer, down a hallway and toward me. I have no idea what to expect from the next hour, or why Derek O'Dell agreed to meet with me.

Two weeks ago I got up the courage at last to email him: "Not sure how to ask this appropriately, if there even is a way," I wrote, "but would you be open to talking with me about your experience on April 16?"

Derek had class on the second floor of Norris Hall the morning of the Virginia Tech shootings and was one of nearly two dozen injured in the attacks that left thirty-three dead, including the shooter, Seung-Hui Cho. I realized that I had been viewing the sadness of this spring somewhat from the outside. I needed the perspective of one who was there, who witnessed the slaughter of classmates and friends and mentors, and who himself had only narrowly escaped death. But why would anyone wish to relive that kind of horror, much less discuss it with a total stranger?

"If you don't want to," I wrote, "no problem at all. If I were in your shoes, I would probably throw a rock at anyone who asked me about that day. The only reason I decided to ask at all is that I've seen you do numerous television interviews and figured you might be willing. If you'd be up for chatting, let me know."

A week passed before Derek responded, every day of which I gradually grew more certain I had offended him, having intruded on a most personal and painful time that was none of my business. *He must be sick of such violation,* I thought, *ready to move on with life as best he can.* I wasn't the media, but I was one more person asking, "What was it like?" Maybe he was simply tired of us all. Who wouldn't be?

A response finally came: "Matt, thanks for your email. I wouldn't mind meeting. How does next Friday, in the afternoon, sound?

He's thanking me? I should be thanking him for not throwing that rock.

The knob jiggles slightly and the door swings in. There in the doorway stands a man I've seen many times in pictures and on TV. Tall, thin, with a gracious smile, Derek reaches to shake my hand and says, "Matt? I'm Derek. It's good to meet you. Come on in. Did you have any trouble finding the place?"

"No, your directions were fine," I say, stepping inside.

"Can I get you something to drink?" Derek asks, soft-spoken. I am struck at once by his humble demeanor. Who is this man who treats me like a welcomed guest in his home, who wants to serve me though he knows I've come to pry into that awful day?

"Water would be great," I answer. I detect in Derek no hint of suspicion as to my motives in coming here. He pulls a glass from a kitchen cabinet, fills it with ice, and hands it to me along with a bottle of water.

"We can talk in here," he says, directing me into the living room. "My roommates aren't home right now."

Sitting on a couch facing Derek, I begin at the only point that seems to make sense: "I'm dying to ask: Why do you agree to these conversations? Why all the interviews you've done? I wouldn't want to talk to anyone."

Smiling, Derek says, "That's funny — I just did an interview for a newspaper, and the reporter there asked me the same thing. I figure if I can help people do their job, I'm happy to."

Is this guy for real? I wonder, disbelieving.

"And," he adds, "it helps me to talk about it."

"Well, if I ask something I shouldn't, just stop me and tell me to move on."

"You can ask anything you want."

For a second, I just look at him, silent, my eyebrows raised. Does he realize how pointed the questions are in my head? Of course, he must. How many times has he been through this routine? "All right, then," I say, taking a deep breath, preparing to dive in. "Can you tell me about that morning?"

"It was unusually cold, and there was a dusting of snow on the ground. My birthday had been just three days before — April 13. I remember thinking that I'd never seen snow after my birthday. I went to Burger King at about 8:40 and then headed to German class in Norris Hall."

"Do you remember what the lecture was on that morning?"

"Yeah. Strangely enough, we were talking about how to quote someone in the media."

"When did you first know something was wrong?" I ask. "Did the shootings start in your room?"

"No. We first saw Cho before the shootings started. He poked his head in our room a couple of times and just looked around. I guess he was scoping out the rooms, planning his attack. The first time he stuck his head in, I just thought he was a student who had got turned around and was trying to find his class. But it seemed strange that he came back a few minutes later and looked in again. That was at about 9:15 or 9:20. The shootings started at 9:41."

A part of me wants to stay and hear what's coming next. Another part wants to run while I still can, before the images described are in my mind for life. But I need to face the world as it is. And it doesn't get more real than this—or more tragic. "What was it like?" I ask.

"The first shots were across the hall, in the hydrology class. It sounded like a nail gun or a hammer hitting concrete blocks. We all looked up, and the professor stopped teaching for a moment, but we just thought it was construction going on next door. They had been working on the building next to Norris all semester. We dismissed it as that.

"Our door swung open next, and Cho walked in. He raised a Glock 9mm handgun and discharged three rounds into our professor, then swung around and fired another eight or ten shots at the class. He reloaded within one or two seconds and fired another ten or so shots while walking around the class."

I feel my forehead wrinkling and face contorting into an anguished form. Derek, on the other hand, appears relaxed, composed. "What was he like as he was doing this?" I ask, almost in a whisper.

"Cho was calm, methodical, not panicked at all."

I can't help thinking Derek could be describing himself, his slow and careful recounting of the carnage. I've heard that people often cannot recall specifics of traumatic events they've experienced; their brains, in a brilliant defense strategy, block the graphic details. For Derek, however, every step Cho took, every shot fired, remains sharp and clear.

"I saw bullets ricocheting off desks and off the wall as he slowly went around the room killing people. He walked down the aisles, putting the gun to people's heads and shooting them at point-blank range to make sure they were dead."

"What were you thinking and feeling?"

"When he came in the room and first started shooting, I thought maybe it was a joke. Until I saw the casings pop out. Then I knew it was real. At first, everyone just froze, trying to understand what was happening. It took a little bit for us to realize this was a shooting, because you just never expect something like that to happen to you. Then those of us who still could began ducking behind desks and trying to move toward the back of the room.

"After Cho emptied the second magazine, the room was motionless and silent, except for a few moans. I guess Cho figured everyone was either dead or mortally wounded, because he left the room at that point and went down the hall to the French class and started shooting there."

"When were you shot?"

"I guess it was as I was going for the floor," he says. "I had my arm up on my desk at first, like this." Derek demonstrates for me the motion he made that morning as he moved to shield himself from the bullets. "I didn't know at first that I'd been shot. My arm just felt numb. It was after Cho left the room that I noticed the blood running from a hole in the arm of my jacket."

"What happened when Cho left the room?"

"Out of about fifteen people in the class, only five of us were conscious. Four of us could stand up. I remember looking around and seeing the face of a classmate who wasn't shot—only two people had not been hit. There was pure disbelief on his face as he was trying to comprehend what had happened. And I was thinking, what should we do?"

"What *did* you do?" I ask.

"I don't think I was in control anymore. It was something else, someone higher up," Derek says, pointing, as if to heaven, to the off-white ceiling of his apartment. "Cho had left the door open, and I sprinted over the tops of the desks to the front of the room and shut the door. I had to go over the desks because there was so much debris in the aisles—book bags, people. I shut the door, and a friend who had been shot in the hand helped me hold it closed. We heard more shots down the hall, maybe fifteen or twenty. Then he came back to our room and tried to get in again. He got the door open three or four inches, but we shut it again. Cho stepped back and started firing at it. The doors in Norris are solid wood, about two inches thick, but the bullets started coming through. Four or five bullets, maybe."

"No one was hit?"

"No, my friend and I were on the floor on either side of the door, holding it shut with our feet. As he was firing at the door, I just started praying to God that we might be saved. Cho left again, and we heard more shots down the hall. Then he came back and tried to get in a third time. Fired two more shots into the door. It was around this time that I heard the shotgun blasts from police officers trying to get in the building on the floor below. Cho had chained the doors. Then I just remember that the shots stopped. Police were on our hall nine minutes after the shootings started. I don't know when Cho killed himself, but it was sometime before the officers got to our floor."

"So you were shot once in the arm?"

"Yeah, the right arm, but there are three bullet holes in the coat I was wearing."

"Three?"

"Hang on, I'll show you."

Derek leaves the room for a moment, then returns holding a thin, black fleece jacket. Putting it on, he shows me the hole from the bullet that pierced his bicep. "It entered here and came out here," he says, pointing to the entry and exit points. "But there is another hole here on the right shoulder. I guess the jacket was raised slightly, because the bullet didn't hit me."

In my mind, I imagine that day, the bullets whizzing all around, barely missing Derek — except for the one.

"There is one other bullet hole in the jacket," Derek says, putting his finger through a small hole in the front of the jacket, next to the zipper. "I didn't even notice it until I got home from the hospital. It's directly over my heart."

Moreover, I notice, it's directly over the silver cross that hangs from Derek's neck. This would seem as good a time as any to ask the question that is foremost in my mind, the reason I contacted Derek in the first place: "What do you think about God after all of this? Does he still seem good to you? What has this done to your faith?"

Without a second's hesitation, Derek answers, "It's strengthened my faith, definitely. The bullet hole over my heart had to have come when I was holding the door with my foot, when Cho was trying to get back in our room. It's the only time I had my jacket unzipped so that a bullet could have come through at that angle without hitting me. And that's the moment when I was praying for God's help."

"But there haven't been any ups and downs to your faith?" I ask, leaning forward from the edge of my couch, fishing for any signs that Derek is glossing over the truth. "You haven't had any questions as to why God would allow this or any trouble experiencing him as good?"

"I've experienced the full range of emotions, for sure: shock, disbelief, grief, survivor's guilt—wondering why I lived when others didn't—but no, it hasn't hurt my faith at all. It's been only positive. People ask, 'Where was God when this happened?' I say he was in that building, because the death toll could have been a lot higher. Cho fired a hundred or more rounds. In our class, five people died, but a lot more could have. And some people who were hurt badly are healing well."

"But," I jump in, "what about those whose prayers were not answered? A more cynical person"—like myself—"might hear your story and think, 'Maybe Derek only experiences God as good because he made it out of Norris with only a wound to the arm.'"

"Although everyone was not saved," Derek responds, "there were a great number of people who, in my mind, would have died without God. My example at the door is just one instance of answer to prayer.

"Take my friend Sean as another example. When I left Norris, I had little hope that Sean would survive. He had been shot in the head. When I made it to the hospital, I began to pray, not for me, but for my classmates this time, and all the others. Specifically, I prayed for Sean. I really didn't think that he was alive, but I still prayed. When the list of deceased students and faculty began to be published, I scrolled up and down, heartbroken as I recognized my classmates' names. Once the toll reached thirty-two homicides and was finalized, I kept searching for Sean's name on the list. It wasn't there. I began looking online to find out more about his status, because at this point, I honestly thought there was a name missing from the list.

I searched for all different phonetic spellings of his last name and finally found that he really was alive.

"In my mind, there is no scientific explanation for that. I literally saw a person get shot in the head, bleed out, and survive. There is no question to me that a good God was there guiding to safety those who survived. And there are other stories of students getting shot four and five times and surviving. Seeing them today, often with little physical scarring—if that isn't God, then I could never come up with any sort of logical explanation for any of it."

I then realize that this is what I've been doing. I've been demanding explanations and answers of Derek. But the question I'm asking has no logical explanation. Can a person experience God as good in the midst of horror and sadness? Derek is saying yes, emphatically. I cannot argue with an experience.

Though I looked for it, I cannot find a hint of bitterness in Derek, only gratitude. "I take every day as a blessing now," he says. "You definitely don't take life for granted after something like this."

I lean back on the couch and notice that the anxious tension I had walking in here is gone. Derek's calm composure has set me at ease. I ask, "In what ways did you experience God as good in the early days after the shootings? What helped?"

"Walking around the Drill Field the day after, seeing the way people were reaching out. It was one of the most moving experiences of my life. People were coming together, hugging, caring for one another, disregarding their differences. There was a sense of not only a stronger community, but a family building and growing. A family that didn't stop with Virginia Tech or Blacksburg—it extended across this nation and even, to an extent, the world. I saw God's family doing what they do best, offering comfort to strangers, embracing the sadness with us, but at the same time hoping and praying for recovery and healing."

Hearing Derek's perspective, I am encouraged by his hopeful response to terror — a word overused these days, but what else would you call what he saw? I find myself thanking God for this hour with Derek. He has experienced the truly awful without having been made awful by it. And he has shown me the possibility of enduring great darkness without losing sight of God's goodness.

Before wrapping up our time, I take a final stab at unearthing any bitterness in Derek: "Do you ever get tired of the marketing of this tragedy, all the T-shirts and signs around campus, plastered with slogans such as We Will Prevail and Never Forget?"

"Nah. I know it bothers some people, but it encourages me to see how this has brought everyone together. The campus and the town are one now. I like seeing that. I want to remember my classmates and my professor who didn't make it. They were everyday heroes to me. I don't want to forget them. I'm trying to live by that motto: Never Forget."

Five

What is it for Derek, after April 16, that makes life more, not less? Why was that sadly not the case for Elie Wiesel, who is "deprived for all eternity of the desire to live"?[8] Like Wiesel, Derek O'Dell will never forget his terrible "night." But for Derek, remembrance brings peace, not despair.

There are, of course, differences between the two tragedies. The slaughter in Norris lasted nine minutes; the Holocaust dragged on for years.

Seung-Hui Cho killed thirty-three people, including himself; Hitler, millions.

Derek prayed for safety, and safety soon came; Wiesel waited years for liberation, which came too late for his family.

Derek acknowledges the death toll in Norris could have been worse; the very term *Holocaust*, by contrast, implies utter destruction.[9]

It would be absurd, if not offensive, to ascribe degrees to suffering. Pain is pain. Death is death. I do not mean one is worse than the other. But I believe Wiesel would say it was the near totality of the Jews' devastation (and that of his family) — and the uninterrupted silence out of heaven — that "murdered my God."[10] Is it possible to experience God as good when life is that bad?

Even the pope sounds uncertain. Visiting Auschwitz in 2006, the site where a million and a half Jews died, he said, "In a place like this, words fail. In the end, there can only be a dread silence — a silence which is itself a heartfelt cry to God. Why, Lord, did you remain silent? How could you tolerate all this?"[11]

When I hear these words and think of the phrase "completely burnt," and when I imagine the smoke Wiesel saw, his flesh and blood rising into the air as ash, I cannot help but think of Mark and Joyce Bryant, only a half hour up the road from Tech, who have known a similar sorrow.

Two years ago, six of their nine children were killed in a gas explosion that obliterated the home of a relative where the kids were spending the night. The tragedy made national news, as did the Bryants' persistent faith through the devastating loss. If anyone could say, "How, Lord, could you tolerate this?" I would think that Mark and Joyce could. And who would blame them? Yet from all the accounts I've read, they have nothing but praise for God. How can this be? How could someone in such a situation have anything other than a grim, grin-and-bear-it belief? Under that degree of pain, how could anyone say, "God is still good; we've tasted and we've seen"?

<hr />

Given the grace with which Derek met my request for a meeting, I should have more confidence in approaching the Bryants. Somehow, though, this call is harder. Several times I reach for the phone, intent on dialing the number, only to slap the phone down on my desk and busy myself with other things till I get up the courage to try again. When I finally go through with it, all my fears are quickly set at ease.

"I think my husband and I would love to talk with you," Joyce says warmly.

The rain is heavy the day we meet. The asphalt is slick, and I take it slow around the twists and turns of the narrow country road that leads to the Bryants' home. "It's a two-story white house," Joyce had said, "set back from the road with a long gravel drive. Look for a maroon tin roof. That's us."

Rushing to the door to avoid being soaked, I am met by Mark and Joyce. They welcome me into their home and lead me into the dining room, where we sit and get to know each other. Eventually we work our way around to the conversation that they, like Derek, must have had with many others before me.

"So how can we help you, Matt?" Mark asks.

I tell them about my role at Tech and about my dad's fall and how that set me on my journey. "I'm wanting to know if it's possible to experience God as good when life isn't. Or is our enjoyment of God dependent on happy circumstances? When life falls apart, can I expect anything more than just a grin-and-bear-it faith?"

"Well," Mark says, "there are days like that, for sure, when grin-and-bear-it is the best one can manage. But God has been very good to us in the past two years since the accident." He reaches for some papers. "Here, I want to read you something. This is from the spiritual journal that Rebekah — our oldest who died — was keeping. She wrote this not long before the accident:

> Lord, your ways are perfect, and you have a plan for me that is just what I need and exactly what you want me to do for you.

You are the one who controls me and what happens to me. You are almighty and never say, "Oops!" Use me today for your will.

"She had completely given her life over to the Lord and was willing to go through anything to be used by him."

"I guess it helps reading something like that?" I ask Mark and Joyce.

"Oh yes," Joyce says. "It's comforting to know all our kids were walking with the Lord. Well, Jackson was two, so he only knew so much, of course. But all our other kids knew the Lord and walked with him."

"By the way," Mark says, lifting his hand and pointing upward, as if just remembering something he meant to say earlier, "I should tell you that you're free to ask anything at all. No question is off limits, so don't worry about that." Joyce nods in agreement.

"Can you tell me about the moment you received the news?" I ask Mark. "Where you were, what you felt? I think that's the moment everyone fears the most—getting the call."

"I was at home with our daughter Kameron who had stayed in Virginia to get work done for school. Joyce and the kids were in Michigan staying with Joyce's sister Lorrie."

"It was Lorrie's home that exploded?"

"Yes," Mark says. "Around five o'clock on a Sunday morning, Kameron woke me up and told me the pastor from church was coming over, that there had been an accident in Michigan. My first thought was that maybe Joyce or one of the kids had been hurt or killed. I told Kameron—who was seventeen at the time—that this couldn't be good and that we needed to prepare our hearts. The pastor doesn't just come over at five in the morning. When the pastor and youth pastor arrived, they told us that Joyce had called and that there had been an accident, a house explosion, that Caleb and Sarah were in the hospital in critical condition, but that the others did not survive."

"What were you feeling and thinking at that moment?" I ask.

"I was just in shock at first. Didn't really feel anything. It seemed like a dream, like I wasn't sure it was even happening. Then Joyce called. I took the phone and walked outside, into the dark, and Joyce said, 'Mark, it's true. There's been an explosion. We've lost six of our children.' And she started naming them off, one by one—Rebekah, Joseph, Nehemiah, Martina, David, and Jackson—they were gone. That's when the grief hit. I went to my knees outside the house and started crying. That morning the pastors rushed Kameron and me to the airport to catch a flight to Michigan, and during the drive, I went into protection mode. I knew I had to gather the family I had left and protect them. I knew they were going to need me now, and I began crying out to God, saying, 'God, I can't handle this! You're going to have to carry me.'"

"Joyce, were you in the house too?" I ask.

"No. My sister Lorrie and I were away at the time of the explosion. We got a frantic call from our sister Katie, who lives next to Lorrie. The scene, when we got there, was horrific. There was no house. There were ambulances and fire trucks, but no house. Not even fire. It was just gone."

Mark shows me a picture of the devastated home, splintered as though a tornado had run over it, debris spread for yards in every direction. "You look at this picture, and you see why it's a miracle that anyone came out alive. There isn't even a refrigerator or stove left in this picture."

"When did you learn which of your children had survived?"

Joyce says, "When we arrived at the scene, I heard bloodcurdling screams that I knew were from our son Caleb. He was terrified and in shock. I got in the ambulance with him and just tried to comfort him. It wasn't until I got to the hospital that I learned who else had survived, that Sarah had made it. I'll never forget that ride, that night. It was such a black night."

"How are Caleb and Sarah now?" I ask.

"They're doing well," Joyce says. "Sarah was very critical when I got to the hospital. She had some broken bones and a punctured lung. But she was not burned. Caleb had flash burns over much of his body, but no internal injuries. Both were able to come home several days after the accident, and they're doing well now."

Mark adds, looking again to the picture, "It's also just miraculous, given the complete destruction of the house, that we were able to have open caskets for all the children except Rebekah. And she was fine. We just figured she would not want an open casket. That there were even bodies for us to bury was a blessing."

"Most of the kids' wounds were internal," Joyce says, "probably from the force of the explosion. The shock was so strong, it knocked a neighbor off his couch."

"I've noticed," I say, "that neither of you has said anything about being angry at God. Mark, you said you cried out to God for help. I'm wondering why you did not lash out at him."

Mark says, "I never felt angry at God, though I think it's fine if other people do. God can take it. But I never felt that. And it never occurred to me that God was punishing our family."

I interject, "But a lot of people *would* entertain such thoughts, that God was angry with them or judging them. How were you able to avoid going down that road of speculation?"

"I think one thing that probably helped," Mark continues, "was that, as a family we had always walked closely with the Lord. Not perfectly, of course, but closely and consistently. We didn't just believe that God was loving — we knew it. And we knew it before any of this happened. Knowing God as good beforehand helped us in knowing God as good afterward."

Glancing at her husband seated next to her, then turning to me, Joyce adds, in full agreement, "When you're in the moment of crisis, you don't whip out your Bible and find a verse. You depend on whatever is already in you. Because we had walked with the Lord beforehand, we had that to draw on. That's why we tell people that it is so important to get to know God every day. No one thinks something like this will happen to them. We didn't either. But when it does happen, you'll be glad you put the time in beforehand to grow that relationship with God."

As I listen to Mark and Joyce, I think of a comment the biblical character Job made after losing all ten of his children. Job *did* wonder whether God was punishing him, and he did go through anger toward God. But no matter how tempted toward despair he might have been, Job could not quite accept the idea that God had become his enemy. Job had a history with God. The two had been friends. And he longed for that sense of closeness in his suffering.

> *Oh, for the days when I was in my prime,*
> *when God's intimate friendship blessed my house . . .*[12]

What if Job had not had such a history with God? Would he have given up?

"It's a choice not to despair," Joyce continues. "It doesn't mean you won't go through depression. It just means you don't despair, which is hopeless. And rather than feeling angry toward God, we've actually learned how much God loves us."

"How so?" I ask, incredulous that anyone could feel more loved by God, not less, after something so terrible.

"We lost four sons," Joyce says, "and now we have only one son, just like God. And I wouldn't give up the one son I have left for anyone. Not for *any*one." Her voice rises with emphasis, and I see from across the dining room table the conviction on her face. "Then I stop and think about God's incredible love in John 3:16. God loved us so much that he gave his one and only Son for us. I understand now something of how awful that must have been for God and what that says about how much he cares for us."

Mark adds, "Another verse that spoke to me was Proverbs 3:5, 'Trust in the LORD with all your heart and lean not on your own understanding.' I'd never read it like this before, but I just felt like this is something I cannot understand, that I have no answers for — but I don't have to. I can lean on his understanding. There really is comfort in that."

"None of this means, of course, that we grieve any less than anyone else would," Joyce says. "Visiting the funeral home and going into the cemetery were awful, beyond words. You see the little bodies, and you want to touch them," she says, reaching out her hands as if to do so, then stopping, "but there's no life in them. If you're not careful, that can bring you to hopelessness. But I remember thinking, even then, 'As bad as this is, there could be something worse.' I didn't have to look at any of my children and wonder where they were. I *knew* where they were. So I grieve, but it's a hopeful grieving. I cry. I wake up in the middle of the night longing for my children. But there is peace."

Mark says, "If God didn't exist, neither would my kids. They'd simply be gone forever. But because he lives, I know they do too."

"Yes," Joyce affirms. "We're stretched between two kingdoms

now. We have kids there and here. We'll stay here as long as God wants us here, but we can't wait to get to the finish line—mostly to say, 'Thank you, Lord!' How hopeless this all would be if our kids were just dead and in the ground. The good news is that we're going to get new bodies."

The Bryants speak with utter sincerity. They do not seem to be saying, "If we don't believe this, what hope will we have?" as if they are simply believing a fantasy for the comfort it will bring. Rather, they are saying, "We *do* believe this—and did before any of this happened—and therefore we have hope."

"What are some specific things," I ask, "that helped you experience God as good in the middle of your grief? How can I know him as good when my turn comes to grieve?"

Mark says, "I'm not sure I have a perfect answer, or if there even is one, because people deal with death differently. But for us, the way people gave was so helpful. Having six funerals at one time is very expensive. The funeral homes helped out, our church was a great source of support, and people around the country just gave so much that we didn't have to pay any of the $80,000 for the funerals. Even the hospital bills were paid for once all the donations had come in."

"And one thing we learned," Joyce says, "is that God doesn't just meet the big needs. He meets little needs too, and those can be just as meaningful. In fact, I would say it's the little, everyday things that count the most. We have so many stories of how God provided little things we needed. I had been thinking how badly the grass needed mowing, and a guy from our church just showed up and started mowing. He didn't say a word to anyone, just got out and started mowing. And I sat staring out the window, crying."

"Then there was the gravel story," Mark joins in. "So many cars had been in and out of our driveway during that time that it had turned to mud and really needed new gravel. We didn't say a word to anyone about it, but a day or so later, a truck pulls up and unloads a pile of gravel for us."

Mark and Joyce look at each other and smile. I can see the pain clearly in their eyes, but I see other things too: joy, gratitude, peace.

Joyce says, "People cooked meals for us and cleaned our house, so we didn't have to worry about all those things we didn't have strength to do. One guy mowed our lawn twice in one week, which it didn't need, but he wanted to help somehow. We have countless stories of the little ways people demonstrated God's goodness to us. On Mother's Day, someone got up before I did and put flowers on each of the kids' graves, so that when I visited the cemetery it was as though the kids themselves were giving me flowers." At this, tears fill Joyce's eyes and quickly slip down her cheeks. "When the apostle Paul says, 'God will meet all your needs' — it's true! And not just the big needs. The small needs too."

As if cued by heaven itself, Mark and Joyce's daughter Sarah, eight years old now, walks up to her mom and gives her a hand-drawn picture that reads, "I love you, Mom." Joyce smiles warmly at her daughter and says, "Thank you, Sarah. Thank you."

This seems a fitting place to close our conversation. I've already taken more of their time than I had said I would. As I stand to leave, Mark gives me a CD of hymns that his daughter Rebekah, the oldest who died, recorded a year and a half before the explosion. And Joyce says, "One more thing that has helped: we were fortunate as a family to have no regrets. We left nothing unsaid. There were no arguments left unresolved. Our kids knew we loved them, and we knew they loved us. So there is sadness, but there are no regrets. And it's wonderful to have that peace."

—

It's raining still. I barely notice though. I'm fixed, instead, on the voice coming from my car's CD player. All the way home I listen to Rebekah Bryant sing of God's grace.

> *When we've been there ten thousand years,*
> *Bright shining as the sun,*
> *We've no less days to sing God's praise*
> *Than when we've first begun.*

Before long, I am singing with Rebekah and pondering what she wrote in her journal: "Lord, your ways are perfect … you never say, 'Oops!' Use me today for your will."

Today, two years since the accident, God is using Rebekah still.

Six

At a funeral, I once overheard a man say, "Why are people crying? We should be celebrating. We're Christians! This man is in heaven." The comment grated on me terribly then. It sounded so spiritual and yet completely wrong. The Bryants' response to tragedy has reminded me why: we may grieve with hope, but we do, and should, grieve.

Standing at the tomb of his friend Lazarus, the Bible simply says, "Jesus wept."[13] I bet he was more than misty-eyed. I bet he bawled. And if Jesus mourned, then mourning is good. If I am to experience a good and sympathetic God in my grief, I must be willing to mourn as well. None of this phony "We're Christians! We should be celebrating" business.

When the apostle Paul said not to grieve as those who have no hope,[14] I do not believe he meant we should mourn *less*, but rather *differently*, without despairing, for we will see our loved ones again. But what an odd thing it would be if the very people who are to be characterized by love — love of God and of each other, the two greatest commands, according to Jesus — did not grieve intensely over death. Indeed, we ought to weep, and all the more, for we have shared a fellowship that is inexpressibly deep.

Jesus again helps me here. In Luke 7 I see him encounter the widow who has lost her only son. Perhaps realizing the pain his own Father would soon feel, he does not scold the lady, saying, "Stop your crying, woman! Don't you know where your son is?" Instead, the Scriptures say, "When the Lord saw her, his heart went out to her and he said" — gently, I think we can assume — " 'Don't cry.' "[15] Then, moved by compassion and into action, Jesus raises the young man from the dead.

The apostle Paul says we can grieve with hope because our sons and daughters shall one day be raised as well. But until then, we *do* grieve, and this is good. Sadness is a sign of love. We hurt because the one who is gone was dear to us. What other response could be more loving than to weep?

Seven

As with the Bryants, it was the little things that comforted me after the shootings here. Many wrote or called, asking how they might help. I assured people that though it might seem like they were doing nothing, the most helpful grace they could give us was prayer. Never had I so sensed the reality of intercession. Many said, and I would agree, that it felt as though we were being held up by others' prayers on our behalf. This was to us a tangible taste of God's goodness during those early days.

There was, however, a darker side to the response, as there always is after a tragedy. Folks who had been students at Columbine during the attack there warned us we'd soon be under an onslaught of Christian (and other) organizations that would come in, uninvited, promoting themselves and telling us how to mourn. Sadly, this was true.

Within days of the massacre, the Drill Field devolved into a zoo-like exhibition of religious oddity. Strange and varied species of faith descended on what had become a sacred spot for grieving students. One could not get near the Hokie stones without first dodging half a dozen representatives of this faith or that, hoping to distribute a tract or booklet. I'm sure most of these groups meant well, but it was hardly the time or place for promoting one's religion. The Virginia Tech community was still in shock, still grappling with the horror that had happened here. A little space and time to process were needed.

Not everyone realized this. One group erected what appeared to be a massive yellow circus tent, round and rising to a point on top, just yards away from the memorial. It looked like a cross between a canvas cathedral and some sort of space rocket. I kept watching to see if it might take off. In the end, it was merely taken down: the eyesore had attracted many stares but few converts.

This group simply misjudged the climate of the campus. This was not Hurricane Katrina. Thousands had not been displaced from their homes, and they had not been abandoned. We still had our community, and it was to our community, to friends and familiar ministers and mentors, that we turned. Few felt as though they had lost everything, and those who did knew where to turn.

We faced a tough challenge convincing some people of this. I spent hours on the phone with groups wanting to fly in and put on an event of some kind. A crisis response seminar. An evangelistic crusade. A concert of healing. At the worst of it, I would hang up my phone, only to have it immediately ring again. My cell phone bill, which normally runs around fifty dollars a month, was, for April, $439.08 — almost none of which was spent talking to students.

One gentleman called to persuade me that we at Tech were unprepared to handle such grief and that we needed his organization's help. He rattled off a list of "big names" in Christianity, the celebrities with whom he was connected. "I can bring to your campus every-body who's anybody in the faith."

"So, the poor?" I said.

I did not actually say that because I didn't think of it until after we had hung up. I did, however, manage to convince the man, and others after him, that no one here was looking for a show, that if a group came in with banners blazing, it would be poorly received by the community. We were very sensitive to the feeling that some were trying to push their way onto the scene, exploiting our sadness for their own self-promotion, turning a massacre into an event.

On a normal day, Virginia Tech is a family. Under these circum-stances, we were inseparable. We did not experience April 16 as a national tragedy, though we were aware of and deeply grateful for the country grieving with us. To us, this was a personal loss, a death in the family, and we mourned it as such.

What we needed most were not bright lights and big names, but simply an arm around the shoulder, a caring word, a heartfelt prayer. Many responded this way. I have a box of sympathy cards in my house, sent by a local Christian radio station. I have yet to read through them all, there are so many.

One man wrote, "We have no answers for your grief. We can only bow our heads and join you in petitions for strength from His Holy Spirit who lives in us." A perfect response. No answers, but an arm around the shoulder. Thank you.

The cards are from all over: "We here in Walla Walla, Washington" — how did Walla Walla hear of a radio station in Virginia? — "want you to know that we are praying for you ... We wanted to reach across these fifty states and give a hug to each of you." That is just what we needed. Again, thank you.

The sweetest comforts in that box of cards are not the words, but rather the pictures, dozens of them, from families and schools and businesses around the country, people dressed in Hokie colors of orange and maroon, holding up signs in support of Virginia Tech. Whenever I look at these pictures, I think of what Paul said in 1 Corinthians 12:26: "If one part [of the body of Christ] suffers, every part suffers with it." Here was the church at its best, saying, "Because you hurt, we hurt too."

And I will always remember one other example of this arm-around-the-shoulder approach. Friday evening of the week of April 16, my church held a time of extended prayer and worship in a place we rent downtown. The room was raw with emotion, the full weight of the week having set in. Sniffles broke the silence between songs and filled the space during prayer. I had cried off and on the whole week, but not as I did this night. The grief kept coming, needing release.

After an hour and a half in this dim, candlelit room that was tear-drenched in sadness, we were led upstairs to another room. Warm chatter and even laughter — I'd forgotten how it sounded — spilled from the doorway into the hall as we approached. And light! Wonderful light leaked from that room, giving the hall a cheerful glow that bid us enter and forget the night.

Once in the room, my eyes fell immediately on a vast spread of desserts, carefully laid out on a long counter. Cookies, cakes, and pies of every sort, every flavor under heaven, it seemed, had been prepared and placed before us. The smell of freshly brewed coffee wafted on the air. Hokie-colored streamers hung from the walls.

A handful of ladies from a church up the road in Salem, Virginia, had spent the day baking; "We had to do *something*," they said. They did not come selling anything, and they were not here to promote their church. They came only to serve, to overcome evil with good.

I tried several times to thank them for the sweet offerings, but I would tear up whenever I went to speak. This simple gesture of love was the first ray of light for me, the first hint of hope, in an otherwise long, dark week. It reminded me life would get better. Life would not be the same as before — it would always be different — but it would not always be like this. Joy and laughter would return. And, in fact, they did return, at least in some measure, that very night.

I tasted more than apple pie that evening. With every forkful I experienced the goodness of God, calling me out of darkness and into marvelous light. I was reminded of a God who did not watch our misery from afar. He brought order and light and love into the very midst of it. It was said of the nations in that day that "the people living in darkness have seen a great light; on those living in the land of the shadow of death a light has dawned."[16]

When my turn comes to comfort others, I hope I remember this: appropriateness counts. No circus tents or big events are needed. An arm around the shoulder will do. By this others will see — will taste and see — that God is good, even when life isn't.

Eight

"God allowed it. He didn't cause April 16, but he allowed it." It's one of those statements that is technically true, but that is so incomplete in and of itself, so lacking in explanation, it sends all manner of wrong signals. When I hear, "God allowed it," as I do a lot these days, I envision the great and powerful President of the planet, with the help of his heavenly aide, running down the docket for the day's events.

> *Aide*: Will there be any plane crashes today, my Lord?
> *God*: Hmmm. No, I don't think so. I won't allow it.
> *Aide*: A student at Virginia Tech wishes to kill himself and thirty-two others.
> *God*: Well, I'm opposed to such behavior, of course. But I'll allow it.

If God is sovereign — meaning there is no authority higher than him — then technically, yes, all things are at the least "allowed."

But to say no more than this is to suggest that God coolly and dispassionately scans the list of possibilities for the day, checking off those he will permit and those he will not. Where in such theology is the outrage of God, his anger toward the evil that mars his good creation? Where is the indefatigable determination to root out all that sets itself up against his dream of love and goodness for the world? Where are the tears Jesus wept for his dead friend Lazarus? Are we to assume that when Jesus was sweating blood in Gethsemane, begging the Father for a way out, God on high looked down with indifference and said, "Sorry, Jesus. I'm allowing it."? Or did he ache with his Son? Did he sweat blood with him? Did he grieve over the lack of alternative options? Yes, in the end, God allowed it. Fine. But he did not do so easily.

We cannot experience as good any God who says okay to tragedy without a stabbing pain in his own heart. And thankfully, we need not try, for this is not our God.

How different is the Lord we find in Scripture from the one we are sometimes presented by well-meaning teachers and preachers, bent on explaining every aspect of God. In Hosea, the lovesick Lover woos a wayward Israel:

> *I will betroth you to me forever;*
> *I will betroth you in righteousness and justice,*
> *in love and compassion.*[17]

Many hundreds of years later, God in the flesh was still wooing, and weeping, for his unrequited love:

> *Jerusalem, Jerusalem, you who kill the prophets and stone those*
> *sent to you, how often I have longed to gather your children to-*
> *gether, as a hen gathers her chicks under her wings, and you were*
> *not willing!*[18]

This is hardly a dispassionate God. This God is more than a laundry list of agreed-upon doctrines, more than a statement of faith I can sign my name to. Ours is a God who is alive, a Being who feels, who experiences joy and pain. He laughs, he cries. If I wish to experience this God as good when life isn't, I must remember to question what I am told of him. Even when the answers are technically correct, much may be missing. What do the answers leave out?

Doctrine is dangerous business. It is *necessary* business — we need to know who it is we worship — but we must define God carefully, allowing for a heavy dose of mystery, which is an inevitable and essential part of relating to the Infinite. We must accept what we do not know and refuse those answers that are hardly answers at all. "God allowed it" may be true enough, but the connotation is utterly false. God is not uninterested in our pain; he hates April 16 more than we do.

So why did he "allow it?" I have no answer. What I do have is an image of the world as it is, an image given in Scripture. We have a planet that was meant for good, but it is temporarily beset by rebellion against its Maker. The result is death and sadness. And it is risky business ascribing the fault for that result — whether determined or allowed — to God.

After 9/11, I asked a well-known preacher why the attack had happened. He knew what I was getting at, that I was asking why God had permitted this. He gently rebuffed me: "I guess I have a pretty simple faith, Matt. I figure if a man flies a plane into a building packed with people, the result will be death, and I don't think that says much of anything about God."

So the world as it is, is not as it should be. Good and evil are at odds, and sometimes evil lands a blow. One day, good will triumph completely. Until then, we lose a battle here and there. As that preacher taught me, such a simplistic worldview can feel rather childish. But I think it is also true. We would do well to embrace it, since it *is* true, and say little else. To go beyond what we know for sure — which, granted, isn't much — is to "allow" for a flood of answers that are *half* true or altogether *un*true, and that will be death to our enjoyment of God. I cannot love a cold, dispassionate doctrine; I *can* love, and experience as good, a God who is Being, who laughs when I laugh and who cries when I cry. This, in the end, is better than answers anyway.

Nine

Are we, then, not safe? Will God not protect us? Perhaps answers are not enough, but a few would be nice, I suppose. A few might even be necessary, for if I answer poorly the question "Will God protect us?" I am risking my enjoyment of God in a crisis.

A few years ago, I wanted to buy a book that was out of print, so I went through a secondhand, online dealer. Before the seller shipped the book, she attached to it a note that read, "Thank you! May you have good health and happiness always." I laughed when I read the note, because the day the book arrived in the mail, I was coming down with a terrible cold.

"May you have good health and happiness always" — a wonderfully kind sentiment, and one that is absolutely not going to happen. I will not always feel good; I will not always be happy; life will contain rough patches; and if Jesus does not return first, I will one day die. We all will. April 16 reminds me of this. Why are we, then, so surprised when it happens?

We Americans have an especially hard time believing constant happiness is not a guarantee. All our lives we've been told by the founding documents of our society that the pursuit of happiness is an inalienable right with which we've been endowed by our Creator. And if God wants us happy, then he must want us safe.

All I need do, however, is stand here on the Drill Field and count the slabs of limestone that lie in remembrance of the dead to know that we are not very safe, that sometimes the pursuit of happiness is frustrated. Most of Seung-Hui Cho's victims were young, having barely begun their pursuit. And some of them professed an active faith.

Lauren McCain, an international studies major and a small group member in my church, wrote in her online Facebook profile, "Religion? It's all about Jesus." If Lauren loved Jesus, why did Jesus not protect her?

I understand the question. I've asked it myself. But I wonder if there are better questions we should ask: Where, in the first place, did we get our belief that faith makes us safe? And is it possible that this expectation of constant happiness comes, not from any promise in Scripture, but from having lived so long in relative peace?

Prior to April, Virginia Tech was a mostly quiet place. I used to say that the worst thing that happens in Blacksburg is that someone has a bike stolen. And for a long time, that was true.

We were used to, and even expected, an easy, safe life in Blacksburg. Then came April 16. We saw that not even our quaint little town is immune from the heavy, sinking sadness of this world. We learned that safety is largely an illusion. We trick ourselves into thinking we're free from suffering, as if pain were something the other poor unfortunate souls of the world must face, but not us.

The Sunday following the massacre, I, along with the other pastors, opened the floor for questions during the service. One student asked, "What do you think about the idea of God's protection in your life? I always believed that when I prayed, God would protect me. So why did the VT students die? If they were Christians and prayed for protection, why weren't they saved?" This student later told me that his mom had said, "I was praying for your protection that morning, so I know if you'd been in that building, you'd have been kept safe."

Really? Can we know that? Is faith a force field protecting us from harm? What, then, of the Christians who died on 9/11? Did they all, in a colossal failure to prepare, forget to pray for safety before boarding their flights or driving into work that morning? Someone, surely, out of all those people, prayed for safe travel and was denied.

I have a friend whose son has just discovered pornography. My friend and his wife wonder why God did not keep their child from this. "We've limited his Internet access; we've prayed for God to protect him from this; why didn't God do it?"

Will God protect me? Will he keep me safe? Can I bank on that? We certainly are not the first to have such a hope. In Psalm 16:1 King David prayed, "Keep me safe, my God, for in you I take refuge." Later, in Psalm 27:5, David seems confident of the protection he sought: "In the day of trouble [God] will keep me safe in his dwelling." God *will*, David says.

But then I look in the book of Job and find cause to question David. Job suffered unimaginable pain. His children, his livelihood, and his health were all taken from him in catastrophic tragedy. His friends came preaching a "God protects the righteous" theology, and God was not pleased. "I am angry with you," God said to Job's friends, "... because you have not spoken of me what is right."[19] The great and terrible irony of Job's life, as we learn from the story, was that he suffered, not because he was bad, but because he was good—*very* good, in fact.

The irony for us at Tech is that after the shootings, I find little anger directed toward Cho, but plenty aimed at God. At first glance, it would appear Jesus overreached, promising us safety he could not deliver. Funny thing, though: I cannot find a single place where Jesus ever promised this much-desired protection. Quite the opposite, in fact: Jesus outright acknowledges the power that people such as Cho have to wreak destruction in our lives. "I tell you, my friends," Jesus says, "do not be afraid of those who kill the body and after that can do no more. But I will show you whom you should fear: Fear him who, after your body has been killed, has the authority to throw you into hell. Yes, I tell you, fear him."[20]

As best I can tell from his words, Jesus seems to say we have too small a goal. We crave physical protection when something greater, of more value, is at stake. Our souls, that part of us which is eternal, which isn't dust and returning to dust, should be our primary concern. To make his case, Jesus begins by saying there *are* some who can kill your body; just don't fear them.

So we are not that safe. Not as safe as we would like to be, at least. Not as safe as David perhaps hoped. And in case we missed his point, Jesus tells his disciples, "In this world you will have trouble."[21] You *will* have trouble: Jesus said this as part of his farewell address to his disciples, and he apparently meant it, because all but one of the apostles were killed for following Jesus. Faith certainly was not a shield against trouble for them.

I wonder if Jesus might say to us, with characteristic compassion of course, "You are angry at me for failing to deliver on a promise I never made. I have not guaranteed your physical safety."

After my friend Baker died at age twenty-five, I knew there was something unnerving about his death. Baker's heart was golden. He was a blameless man. Not perfect, but blameless, a shining example of a Christ-follower whose desires seemed to be for all the right ambitions. If God would want anyone to live, surely Baker qualified. Surely a man with a mission like Baker's would not be bested by leukemia. Surely a smile like his doesn't die easily. Yet Baker is dead. And his grave ought to give unrest to us all and shake us from our arrogance. If Baker could die, so can, and will, we all. None of us can be complacent. None of us is "safe." It should give us pause to think that one so full of life is gone — and so quickly.

I have that same feeling, that same reaction, visiting Matt La Porte's grave. The only risky thing he did that morning was get up and go to class. What prevents me from joining him in death today? Tomorrow? Does *anything* prevent it?

The world that is does not permit a guarantee of protection. Evil and its counterpart, death, do not allow for that possibility. And if I demand from God what he has not promised, I risk corrupting my faith with bitterness and resentment when God fails to come through as I feel he should. I will never experience God as good in my pain if I am forever suspicious of his having allowed my pain in the first place. Baker knew physical safety was no guarantee. Thus, he was never angry at God. Rather, he experienced God as deeply, wonderfully good, right to the end.

A little more than two months before Baker's death, he and I spoke openly of the what-ifs. What if the bone marrow transplant failed? What if he caught a bug of some kind while lacking an immune system capable of fighting it? (Which is, by the way, what happened.) I will always remember the peace with which Baker spoke of his own encroaching mortality. He knew death was a real possibility. But he also knew what Jesus had said, that there was a higher goal than physical safety, that leukemia had power, perhaps, in this life, but no further. And he knew what Jesus had *not* said, that safety was ever a guarantee. Baker, therefore, made no demands of God and felt no bitterness when the demands went unmet. He remained his joyful self, whether sick or well.

Whenever I visit my hometown, where my friend is buried, I stop by his grave to grieve. I mourn the devastation that decay is slowly bringing upon his body. I'm not okay with it, and I never will be. But nowhere on earth do I experience such certainty of the coming resurrection, when death will no longer sting, as I do at Baker's grave. He left for me a legacy, an example of experiencing God as good when life is at its worst. When my time comes, may I too have a higher goal than safety.

Ten

So God doesn't promise blanket protection. All right. But then all seems random. It could have been any building on campus, any classroom of students. The Christians weren't kept safe, nor were they the only ones taken. As with life, so with death: some were Christians, and some were not. Why? Why those students and not others?

We're uneasy with randomness. Our faith does not permit a world of mere chance. We want to find a reason, a plan, that explains or gives purpose to the death of those particular victims. We want to know there was divine intent behind it all. But what if we just can't know a reason why?

In the Old Testament, after his children died, Job looked for—at times even demanded—an explanation. He received none. The only reason we can find for his misery is that he was the most righteous of all men, and that made him a target for Satan. That does not, however, explain why his kids were killed, why God permitted the collateral damage of ten children to prove a point. Whatever the point, whether to prove God's worth or Job's perseverance, or both, or neither, ten kids died to make it. Why? How did God arrive at the conclusion that it was worth it? We don't know, and God doesn't explain himself. Rather than giving answers, God asks Job more questions.[22]

Because we don't like not knowing the answers, and because we assume our faith always provides them, we end up spouting faulty theology. We say things like, "I was praying for your protection, so I know if you'd been in that building, you'd have been kept safe." That isn't true, but we don't know *why* it isn't true. It is a mystery, and we're not okay with that. I don't know why Baker is dead and I'm alive, though he was twice the man I am.

Did God wish to stop the killings but could not? That thinking seems totally out of step with Scripture. God set limits on what Satan could do to Job. But why did he set them where he did? And why the seeming lack of limits altogether for Job's children? We don't know, and the answers theologians give us sound hollow, as though we're trying to get God off the hook for running the world in ways we don't like.

Accepting that we do not know why — not really, anyway — is a strange feeling. And strangely freeing to me. I'm free to be human, with all its limitations, and free not to be God with all his responsibility. He can be the Sovereign and I the servant. I do not always have to explain. I can live without knowing.

After the death of her husband to cancer, Madeleine L'Engle writes, "We do not have to understand God's ways, or the suffering and brokenness and pain that sooner or later come to us all. But we do have to know in the very depths of our being that the ultimate end of the story, no matter how many aeons it takes, is going to be all right."[23]

Embracing mystery brings peace.

Eleven

People often ask, "What are you writing? What's your book about?" Upon telling them, I typically get a two-pronged response. First, a bewildered look, then a suggestion: "Why not write something happier?" I'm sure I will someday, but for now, these are the matters that consume me: life and death, joy and pain, how our world can be, in the same instant, a place of beauty and horror.

"Why not write something happier?" We are always running from death, from even the mention of it. I want, instead, to run right up to the edge of it this summer, to see what I might see. To learn something from it. We cannot have only sunny days and the sensation of bliss. That is not the world we live in. I am newly awakened to reality this summer and feel an intense need to live in it, to speak truthfully about existence and about death.

A few years back, a friend of mine lost her dad after heart surgery. Doctors had warned the family to be prepared. His heart might simply give out. The surgery, however, went fine. The problem came afterward, when a blood clot gathered and lodged in his brain, causing an aneurism. The vascular explosion in the man's head left him brain-dead. His daughter, my friend, said, "The irony was watching his heart, which we had thought would be the problem, beat on and on for several minutes after the machines keeping him alive were turned off."

At the funeral home, I overheard a man, still in shock, I suppose, speaking in a very present-tense manner of all the things he and my friend's dad "are going to do." My friend, by contrast, spoke with utter clarity, absolutely truthfully, no denial in her words: "Dad was one of my best friends. I know I will see him again, but I'm going to really miss him."

She was soon back at work. "Dad would have wanted me to return to work as soon as I could." And though she grieved, deeply I would imagine, she said, "I have not had any trouble sleeping at night. I'm not angry at God. I've actually felt God very close to me through this."

She embraced and grieved the world as it is, in all its sadness, and that choice made the difference. She did not pretend the world was fine when it wasn't. She didn't expect life to bring only happy days. She lived in reality, not demanding from God a pain-free journey that God had not promised. And so she was prepared, able to taste and see that God is good. I feel a call to live this way now. I want to know, when the phone rings, and the news is bad, that I'll respond as well.

Down the street, across from my house—on the corner adjacent to the cemetery—sits an apartment complex full of those students who have remained in Blacksburg for summer classes. At night, I can hear wild hoots and hollers from drinking parties that have resumed. They ceased for a while after April 16, when people were dragged out of unreality, out of avoidance, into the world as it is. For a time, it seemed we were truly human. We were polite to one another, walking softly around broken hearts amid a pain so piercing one could not block it out.

But a little time has passed, and some here *have* now begun to block it out. Some seem to have forgotten that mournful march into the cemetery for Matt. In fact, they seem to have forgotten the cemetery altogether, and how it sits, very near, as a constant reminder that our stay here on earth is short — that we ought to do something with life while we have it, rather than drinking ourselves into a stupor so strong we forget we're alive at all. If the phone rang tonight, would we be ready to deal with the world as it is? Are we living in reality?

"How many of us really want life," Madeleine L'Engle writes, "life more abundant, life which does not promise any fringe benefits or early retirement plans? Life which does not promise the absence of pain, or love which is not vulnerable and open to hurt? The number of people who attempt to withdraw from life through the abuse of alcohol, tranquilizers, barbiturates is statistically shocking."[24]

Twelve

Madeleine L'Engle is something of a sage for me. I do not always agree with her, but I am always made better by her. Though best known for her children's fiction, such as *A Wrinkle in Time*, it is her nonfiction that most stirs and affects me.

I discovered her work years ago during a time of significant doubt and questioning. Her book *Walking on Water* helped me move beyond my impasse. She writes of her own struggles:

> I had been reading too many theologians ... I was at a point in my life where my faith in God and the loving purposes of Creation was very insecure, and I wanted desperately to have my faith strengthened. If I could not believe in a God who truly cared about every atom and subatom of his creation, then life seemed hardly worth living. I asked questions, cosmic questions, and the German theologians answered them all—and they were questions which should not have been answered in such a finite, laboratory-proof manner ...

The anonymous author of *The Cloud of Unknowing* writes, "By love God may be gotten and holden, but by thought or understanding, never."

Love, not answers.[25]

For a would-be-one-day pastor, this was invaluable wisdom. Sometimes answers are not enough. When such days come, I must taste and see something better than explanation.

I am returning to Madeleine L'Engle this summer. She refuses to live in unreality, insisting instead on embracing the world as it is and speaking truthfully of it, the good and the bad. She writes, "I am acutely uncomfortable when people talk about 'passing away' because they're afraid to say 'die.' When I die, I will die; I won't pass away, or pass on, or pass out. I will die."[26]

I remember feeling this same acute discomfort with the way people spoke of April 16, the way they sometimes still do. Countless spokespeople for one or another organization talked of the "deceased." This sanitized term lessens, I suppose, the sting of such a word as "dead," but it is also less real. When my friend Baker succumbed to leukemia, I did not think of him as "deceased." He was horribly dead. When the call came from my mother, I was not concerned that perhaps my dad might "expire." I was worried he would die. We need a God who deals in reality, in death, not expiration.

Yet I too try to water down the pain. I am guilty of this same insistence on using euphemisms. When the news outlets began reporting the "Virginia Tech *massacre*," I balked. "Tragedy" felt more appropriate, less flashy, less an obvious attempt to garner ratings. You might say "shootings" when you'd said "tragedy" too many times, but "massacre"? Seemed a bit over the top.

I am realizing, though, that the media got it right. I had it wrong.

April 16 *was* a massacre. While I would not presume to speak for anyone else, I believe my own insistence on less graphic terms was a means of dulling the pain, denying the bitterness of the moment. *Come on, it wasn't a* massacre; *it wasn't* that *bad.*

I bet the families of the victims think this was more than a "shooting" — what a pitifully anemic word to describe what happened. I bet the first responders who came upon the carnage would opt for terms stronger than "tragedy," if they'd even speak of what they saw.

Thirteen

Another example of this refusal to live in reality is the reaction to Cho's rampage. At first, thirty-two stones were placed in a makeshift memorial to those killed. Soon, however, someone added a stone for Cho. Next to it lay a note that read, "I'm sorry we couldn't help you."

I am bothered by this expression, by what it implies. I'm bothered by the thirty-third stone, by the subtle suggestion that there is no difference between Cho and his victims. Word got out quickly that Cho was mentally ill. The state declared him so, the media reported it, and from then on, Cho was just another victim. He couldn't help it, some said. "It's not his fault. He was sick." Reporters called Cho "troubled" and wondered aloud why more wasn't done to help him. "It's the mental health community's fault," we were told. "Blame them." Or maybe the school administration is at fault. Maybe they should have better heeded the doctor's warnings.

Cho gets a pass; everyone else is suspect. This seems utterly unfair, as does the attempt to place Cho on the same level with those he killed. I'm grateful for such a forgiving community. I'm honored to be among them. And I respect the good intentions of the one who added the thirty-third stone. But Cho *is* different from his victims. He is the reason for the other stones. He is the reason we cry. We may grieve his loss — every life is precious, of course — but the stones are a memorial, and we do not memorialize evil. We do not honor it. One does not visit the Holocaust museum expecting a tribute to Hitler. He forfeited his honor by his atrocities. He cannot blame an illness for his actions. He is culpable, what he did was evil, and we do not memorialize it.

That word, *evil*, is out of place in this climate. No one wants to say it. My copastor Jim told a reporter on the evening of April 16 that events like this confirm for him what our faith teaches, that evil is real. "It's not just a theological concept, ethereal and weightless. Evil is a concrete reality, and it paid us a visit today."

Jim's comment aside, I have not heard the word *evil* used one time to describe Cho's actions. Thirty-two people were slain by a man who then killed himself, and no one wants to say it was "wrong." Wrong implies moral responsibility, and we're not allowed to suggest that. "He couldn't help it; he was sick." What good can come of a people who stare evil in the face and turn to blame themselves: "I'm sorry *we* couldn't help you"? The intention is pure, I know. And again, I am proud to be among friends so forgiving. But can we truly forgive what we have never said was wrong? Can our mercy be anything but a hollow pleasantry until we have acknowledged the crime committed? Can we experience God as good when we aren't even clear on what good is (and what it isn't)?

We cannot always blame our influences or our sicknesses. "The devil made me do it" will not wash. I do not think, when pondering the practice of slavery, "Well, it was just their culture back then." Slavery *was* their culture, their common practice—and perhaps for that reason few questioned it—but it was more. It was evil. And we must call it so. To do otherwise, to give evil a pass, to blame our influences and our sicknesses, is to reduce behavior to amoral activity. *Murder* becomes a term of absurdity. We cannot say thirty-two were "murdered." We have to say thirty-three "died." "Murder" implies a choice: someone killed when he could have let live.

Madeleine, my sage, would not accept such nonsense, and neither can I. I cannot accept an amoral world or an existence void of personal responsibility. It is a lie, as was the idea that we were ever truly safe. Such a world doesn't exist. Faced with this realization, I can shrink from reality, drink myself into oblivion, perhaps. Or I can embrace the world that is, grieve its brokenness, and live healthily. Avoidance, the refusal to speak truthfully, brings only absurdity, like a stone to honor Cho.

For weeks, and maybe months, Cho pondered and planned his attack. That is evil, and we must say so. If ever there was a time to speak honestly about our world, this is it. To do so is scary, I know. We open ourselves to dangerous possibilities. To acknowledge another's evil is to tempt ourselves toward all manner of wrong response: bitterness, self-righteousness, even hatred. I'm thankful our community has avoided all these, but only once we've called evil what it is can we truly forgive.

One night, when visiting the stones, I noticed a name was missing. *Whose is it? I count thirty-two.* Seung-Hui Cho's was missing. The inevitable had happened. The thirty-third stone had been stolen. *How did they get it away?* The place was never vacant; mourners came day and night. *Someone had to see it being taken.* A letter soon appeared in the school newspaper, its author "saddened and outraged" at the stone's removal.[27] We do not choose our family, the writer said. Cho did a bad thing, but he was a Hokie, he was family, she argued.

I can appreciate the sentiment but not the logic. "We lost 33 Hokies," the letter said, "not 32." Yes, thirty-three *died*, but thirty-two were *killed*. We have to make that distinction or we're back to absurdity.

"I mourn the loss of his young life," the letter said of Cho. "I mourn a society that was so disinterested in this human life." The devil made him do it! The community is to blame!

We have to stop this. I cannot run slow drivers off the road because they anger me — and they do very much — then pass it off as society's fault. I am not marginalized; I am not a victim. I am a moral being, as was Cho, who must own his actions.

But the letter did its work. The next night there were thirty-three stones again, and there have been ever since. So be it. I suppose, forced to choose, this extreme is better than the other. Better to give a pass than to refuse forgiveness.

Fourteen

Never will I forget the smell of the Drill Field by dark in the early days after April 16. Dozens of scented candles, placed among the stones, filled the air with irony: *Why should a place of death smell so sweet?* So many candles burned here that the aroma wandered far, presumably past the crime scene tape, up the steps of Norris Hall, and into classrooms silent after chaos. Those candles became an icon for me: When surrounded by death, can my experience of God smell as good?

The candles have all burned out, though; the sweetness has gone out of the air. Flowers have wilted and browned, and this memorial sits as a scar on the face of my home that will never be the same. This may be what stings the most, that this little town I have loved so much has been forever changed. It cannot go back to the way it was. Is this how the garden felt after Adam and Eve fell? One man's evil ruined that place, and the same is true here.

Though I try, I cannot quite remember the old feelings I once knew, walking around this campus at night. I'll never pass by Norris now without thinking of what happened there. The orange glow from the old iron lampposts somehow looks less warm. It's all so unfair. One man took from us our home.

I need out. Out of this town, for a little while at least. I need to remember the world that was, a world before we knew such a heavy, sinking sadness.

Part 2

Echoes of Eden

Remembering the World That Was

One

We move toward whatever has our attention.

Awhile back, I was driving through the Virginia mountains at sunset. I came around a curve in the road, and there, off to my left, suspended just above the Blue Ridge, was a perfect circle of deep orange blaze, burning up the early evening sky. Thick summer haze muted the sun's usual brilliance so that I could safely stare straight into it.

My heart was in my throat at the sight, and my whole body seemed to swell at this unexpected glory, dangling like a carrot in front of me, enticing me in. Whatever had been on my mind a second earlier was utterly gone, lost in sudden beauty. I must have leaned into it, because I happened to glance at the road and saw that I had drifted precariously across the yellow line and into oncoming traffic. Snapping into action, I jerked the wheel (and the car) toward safety. The car in front had slowed to a crawl and was likewise drifting and jerking, drifting and jerking, over and over again, suffering the same distraction. And every time I looked off to my left to catch the sun sinking into the tree line, threatening a forest fire, I was drawn in, moved in its direction.

—

I come to the North Carolina coast for a conference, two sermons I am to give on the topic of community; at least, this is my excuse. I jumped at the offer to speak, drawn to the sea by remembrances. When I was a child, my family spent summer vacations at the beach, and something in the salt and sand of those memories draws me to the shore. I am reminded of a time when life was simpler, a time long before April 16, when all I had to do was splash and play all day.

I step into the surf. Sea foam surges past my feet, then slows, grasping at land, pausing to wrap my ankles in froth before slipping back out to sea. With every crash upon the shore, the tide pushes closer to the dunes. I wade farther out, the sea, warm like bathwater, up to my knees now. A high and mischievous wave rushes past, splashing up the khaki shorts I had meant to keep dry. I jump to avoid a drenching and laugh. *Oh well, it's just water.*

The ocean breeze brushes over my face, carrying comforting scents of salt and seaweed and whisking away the sadness of this spring. A little way out, a flock of pelicans, like kamikaze pilots, soar high into the air, then turn and fall beak-first, dive-bombing the surface of the sea in search of food. I watch for several minutes as they repeat the maneuver again and again with grace and precision.

The sun is low and to my back as it begins its retreat for the night, casting the water before me in gray-green tones. I stare at the point where sea meets sky as though, if I only look far enough, I can see God on the other side staring back at me and smiling as I am smiling. I am drawn toward the horizon, toward the Maker of this beauty. My heart wells up, and I cannot keep from singing with the psalmist, "Let heaven and earth praise him, the seas and all that move in them."[1]

This is why I've come to the coast: not to speak, but to remember, to be reminded. It is here that I am stilled enough to listen. Here at the edge of North Carolina, I catch echoes of the way the world once was, the way it was intended to be for all time, splashing and surging and soaring with its Creator. Eden is gone, but on evenings like this, with waves crashing at my feet, I can still hear its song, I can sense its peace, and I am drawn in.

Creation is a strange but potent balm for grief, better than any answers I could give. Why did God let April 16 happen? Why Columbine? Why did he not prevent the Holocaust, or at least end it? Why did we have to end it, and the whole war, ourselves, and with the horrors of the atomic bomb? (The pictures of charred children after the blasts are with me for life.) I do not know the answers to these questions, and even if I did, I bet they wouldn't satisfy.

I do not need one more sermon assuring me God is good. I need to taste and see this for myself. And so I go to nature, am drawn into its wonders, where my questioning finally ceases. Here I am able to obey the instruction "Be still, and know that I am God."[2] This has been my practice since my early twenties, during a time of serious depression and spiritual doubt. Growing up, I preferred the city and things of man. I never liked the woods, never understood why my dad did. But when the dark time came, and the lights of heaven seemed to go out, it was under a forest ceiling that I found a measure of peace.

I remember, in particular, one winter walk through Jefferson

National Forest. Poverty Creek ran cold and clear, icy along the edges. A narrow, muddied path stretched out in front of me, weaving its way through naked trees. The ground was covered in the aftermath of fall, a blanket of browned and brittle leaves. Diffused light of an overcast afternoon gave the sky a cheery yellow tint. And except for the sound of passing cars from a nearby highway, the air was silent and still.

What simple glory all around! How had I missed it until now? In contrast to the chaos in my mind, I found here in nature a world of intricate order and design, a place seemingly untouched by all that had gone wrong on the earth, and in my life. Here, all was as originally intended. Depression had dulled my image of God, flattened him, drained him of any color or wonder or beauty. He was reduced to mere doctrine, to a gray idea or abstraction. But out here! Out here was a God of exuberance for life, teeming with color and personality, bursting with joy and affection, with a thirst for all things good. Where had this God been all my life? He'd been there all along, drawing me into the woods, calling me to retreat from the things of man, if only for a while.

My depression gave way over time.[3] My habit of retreating never did. I still hunger for those moments alone in nature, and so I accept invitations to speak at conferences on the coast, simply so I may get out among the creation. Creation itself is not the thing. But it speaks to us of that which is. It tells us of a good God who long ago made the heavens and the earth and saw that it was good.[4]

In Scripture, before God ever reveals himself as Father, Savior, Redeemer, he first reveals himself as Master Artist, beginning with nothing and making of it everything, so that when I step outside, I am stepping onto his canvas. Simple things reveal to me his heart and mind: frosty yellowed grass crunching underfoot in January;

dewdrops dangling from slender threads of spiderweb on an early May morning; the sweetness of roses permeating the hot and heavy summer air; a spray of autumn color just before the trees let go their leaves.

As author Michael Card says, "A thousand examples speak of a deep, inner hunger for beauty that, at its heart, is a hunger for God. We hunger for beauty because it is a beautiful God whom we serve."[5]

I see God's reflection in the sea this summer. When August comes, I'll taste him in the wild, juicy blackberries back home. And I'll know from this that he is good. I'll taste it; I'll see it. He is not the author of April 16. I do not know why such tragedies happen, or why he bids the world go on like this for so long. But standing in the surf, gazing at the horizon, I am moved out of grief and toward faith and hope. I am pulled toward a peace that surpasses understanding. I am stilled enough to catch the echoes of the world as it once was. Eden is gone, but reminders of it—and of its good Designer—are all around.

Two

We no longer sing about creation. The hymns of old were full of allusions to nature and of its power to move us toward God.

> This is my Father's world,
> The birds their carols raise,
> The morning light, the lily white,
> Declare their Maker's praise.[6]

I am glad my generation has taken the psalmist to heart in singing to the Lord new songs. The Master Artist is always inspiring fresh art; we need not only sing hymns. But where in our novelty is that age-old awe at creation?

> This is my Father's world:
> He shines in all that's fair.
> In the rustling grass I hear him pass;
> He speaks to me everywhere.[7]

Does he still speak to us in this way? Would we hear him if he did? What has happened to our wonder? Have we forgotten that balm for grief our ancestors knew?

> *This is my Father's world.*
> *O let me ne'er forget*
> *That though the wrong seems oft so strong,*
> *God is the Ruler yet.*[8]

This spring has made it easy to forget. It is hard to imagine God as Ruler of anything after a time of tragedy. What was he doing the morning of April 16? September 11? Any and every day in Iraq? In contrast to those old hymns, the whole universe appears rather unruly, and the one who could set it right seems unwilling to do so. Could this be why we no longer sing? We feel the disconnect between our right answers and our actual experience.

Some days it takes a monumental leap of faith to believe in a good and strong Ruler. Some days I simply cannot get there. Until, that is, I stop trying to work it all out in my head. Until I, instead, do as the hymn-writer suggests: move toward creation, let it draw me out of intellectualism to use my senses, to taste and see that the Lord is good.

I come once more to the edge of the Atlantic, this time at night. I lay on the shore, brushing away sand crabs looking for a midnight snack. Darkened waves I cannot see rush and roar. Overhead, the sky is a window. Through it I see a billion points of light or more, and, stretching across the heavens, the blotchy haze of the Milky Way.

The vastness of the universe, and our relatively small place in it, quickly sets in. I open to wonders I cannot fully fathom. Our sun, which is hiding right now, is 93 million miles from earth, yet by day it can burn me in fifteen minutes. And even at such distance, the sun is 270,000 times closer than the next nearest star. Besides the sun, our galaxy consists of 200 billion stars, which seems enormous enough until I consider that according to some scientists, there are as many galaxies in the universe as there are stars in the Milky Way. Our "closest" neighbor, the Andromeda galaxy, is 2.2 million light-years away! It is but a faint blur in the sky above me tonight, the light of which left Andromeda 2.2 million years ago. *How do I know it's even still there?*

Farther out, and somewhere overhead, drifts the majestic Sombrero galaxy, or Messier 104 (M104), in NASA language. I've read about this heavenly wonder: "The galaxy's hallmark is a brilliant white, bulbous core encircled by the thick dust lanes comprising the spiral structure of the galaxy."[9] Because we view Sombrero at an angle that is almost edge-on, the galaxy appears to us in the shape of the famous hat for which it's named.

At a distance of 28 million light-years from earth, the galaxy is too far out to be viewed by the naked eye, but the Hubble snapped a shockingly detailed "close-up" picture that I once tried to set as my computer's desktop wallpaper.

The computer locked up. The resolution was too great. Imagine: an image of the thing so large, my nearly new computer could not contain it. And the thing itself? Fifty thousand light-years across and equal in mass to 800 billion suns.[10]

And still pathetically small: Sombrero is only one of 200 billion such specks in the universe, like flecks of glitter flung from God's hand. By some estimates, the universe — how does anyone know this? — extends for trillions of light-years, only 46.5 billion of which we can see.[11]

Stop! I cannot take it all in.

I lay on the sand, at first humiliated by our terrible smallness, then greatly comforted. Perhaps the universe is all right after all. Perhaps the infection is limited to earth. And if so, then our little planet, with its voracious appetite for violence, is but a drop of disobedience in God's vast and otherwise harmonious sea. For all we know, the rest of creation goes on according to its good design; Andromeda and Sombrero might say they're doing just fine, thank you very much.

We have not ruined everything. We are not big enough to do so, and there is some hope in this: "God is the Ruler yet." And if he is the Ruler, then I can truly believe this spring—this *world*, this tiny speck in the far-flung creation—will have a resolution, somewhere down the road.

At last I am singing with the stars and with the saints of old.

> *This is my Father's world:*
> *Why should my heart be sad?*
> *The Lord is King; let the heavens ring!*
> *God reigns; let the earth be glad!*[12]

Three

I am invited by some coastal residents to a cookout. I cannot wait to go, to see what type of people live surrounded by the sea and all its wonders; people who are constantly catching echoes of the beautiful world God intended. Surely such glory is contagious; it must rub off on folks.

When I get there, however, I am shocked, absolutely horrified, by the behavior of a longtime resident. The man yanks one of his daughters by the arm, holding her up for his buddies to see. "Look at these legs!" he says, laughing, pointing to the tiny limbs scarred by scraped mosquito bites. "My daughters look like refugees!" Everyone laughs, except the little girl, who cannot be more than ten. She only looks down at the ground, embarrassed, as her dad goes on. "Who's that TV preacher on Sunday mornin's beggin' for money? That Feed the Children preacher? I should send him a picture of my girls and have him send me food."

I cannot help but notice that all the men, save for the frail guy basting the barbecue chicken, are greatly overweight. Awful, angry thoughts fly through my mind. *I imagine that preacher has to beg to get you away from the grill. Pictures of starving kids aren't enough.*

The man turns to his son. "Boy, take your sisters inside and tell your momma that if she lets them out again, she and I are gonna have a conversation." *Lord only knows what a "conversation" would entail.*

Before the boy — maybe thirteen or fourteen years old — can get up, one of his sisters grabs a canoe paddle and slams it down on her brother's right hand, resting on the arm of his lawn chair. Understandably, the boy has to fight back tears from the pain. I look to the dad, wondering what barrage of insults he has lined up for his disobedient daughter. Instead, the man laughs wickedly and ridicules his son: "What, you gonna cry like a little girl? Look, my son's a little girl."

I keep waiting for someone to speak up, to chastise the dad, to defend these helpless kids. I keep wondering why I do not.

The boy's granddad speaks: "If he's gonna stay here all summer, he's gonna leave a *man*." Apparently men don't cry when whacked full force across the knuckles with a paddle.

Lost on these men is the irony of Culture Club playing in the background on the radio station they chose. *Men shouldn't cry, but you can listen to Boy George?*

I fade from the conversation for several minutes, utterly disillusioned, fighting off all the nasty things I'd like to say. *How can this be? These people live surrounded by beauty, but it hasn't done a thing for them, hasn't helped them at all.*

I come to again, just in time to hear the dad say, bitterly, to one of his friends, "I haven't spoken to my father in thirty years, not since he and Mom got divorced."

Of course. My seething turns to sadness, then to compassion, as I realize how this man got this way. He's only teaching his kids what he learned from his own dad. He's just passing on his wound. I do not know now if glory is contagious, but evil certainly is. From generation to generation it spreads in front of me, an infection so strong, beauty alone is not a cure.

I have sometimes wondered since April 16 — at sundown when the sky is on fire, or evenings staring at the stars — whether Seung-Hui Cho could have killed thirty-two people, and then himself, had he only known beauty. But of course, maybe he did. Maybe he, like this angry, damaged dad, saw the Carolina shores. Maybe he hiked the Colorado mountains. Perhaps he even stood on the edge of the Grand Canyon.

On a clear night, we walk beneath the stars, a billion galaxies hanging over our heads. How many of us stop to marvel? Do we even notice? We go on our way none the wiser, more enticed by the latest fashion trend. We'd rather see a movie than a shooting star.

The mere presence of beauty is not enough to heal us. We must move in its direction, let it capture our attention, choose to be drawn in. The instruction to "taste and see" implies a decision on our part. It's a choice to taste the goodness of God in the sweet blackberries back home. I must look for the Lord's reflection in the sea; otherwise, all I see is water.

The apostle Paul said, "For since the creation of the world God's invisible qualities — his eternal power and divine nature — have been clearly seen, being understood from what has been made, so that people are without excuse."[13] Clearly seen. It's there. It's all around. We simply have to want it, have to choose to taste and see it.

I recall that many years ago, as I was wrestling depression and my doubts about God in the woods of Jefferson Forest, I walked the trails below the trees and pondered Isaiah's words, "Holy, holy, holy is the LORD Almighty; the whole earth is full of his glory."[14] *Why can't I see it, God? Isaiah says it's everywhere, that the earth is filled with it. But I just don't see it. Help me see your glory, God.*

What was I expecting? What did I think glory looked like, anyway? An energy of some sort? Some supernatural light that would appear and cover everything? I did not know. I only knew I needed healing and that a loaded term like *glory* seemed a good place to start. In the end, I saw nothing that wasn't already there, only things right under my nose that I'd somehow never noticed: the invisible qualities of God displayed in the visible world he made.

I wish this damaged dad could know, wish I would find the nerve to tell him: *Look to the sea! Its power and glory are a glimpse of God's! There's healing in this beauty, and it's all around you. Taste it, see it!*

But of course, he *can* know it. Paul says it is clearly seen, so that we each are without excuse. The psalmist says, "The heavens *declare* the glory of God."[15] They shout it out. We must simply give attention and be drawn in. The choice is ours to hear the echoes, to heed the call: when life isn't good, taste and see that the Lord is.

Four

I am learning to heed, making the choice to hear. I am listening long for echoes this summer, straining to hear even faint whispers of the world that was, and of its good God.

I have said previously that we cannot have only sunny days and the sensation of bliss, that this is not the world we live in. That is true. But here by the sea, I realize that the inverse is also true. The real world I am seeking to engage, to embrace, is not solely a place of dust and ash. Life is more than deathly sting, more than a mournful march, even after April. And so I cannot live only by a graveside. I cannot linger too long by Baker's tomb; he would not want me to. It is good to grieve, but also to smile.

> *To every thing there is a season . . .*
> *A time to weep, and a time to laugh*[16]

So I must think and speak truthfully about the bad in life, of course, but also the good. And there is a lot of good. There is beauty cast about everywhere I look.

As Madeleine L'Engle's husband lay deteriorating from cancer, drifting downward toward death, she sat on her porch one evening and wrote of the sky at twilight: "The clouds are achingly beautiful.... I am deeply, piercingly rejoicing in the beauty."[17] Even as her husband slipped from the world, and from her reach, L'Engle did not lose her taste for, or her determination to see, creation's wonder around her. Heartache and beauty, the good and the bad: she gave attention to both, and so avoided despair.

As the apostle Paul wrote, "Whatever is lovely, whatever is admirable — if anything is excellent or praiseworthy — think about such things."[18] I imagine he means to dwell on them: one translation says to "fix your thoughts"[19] on good things. What might have become of that wounded, bitter dad by the shore had he done so?

This is not avoidance. It is simply being fair with existence. The world is awful, yes, but it is not *only* awful. It is wonderful as well. It is teeming with the leftovers, surviving reminders of an original design that was lovely like its Creator. To dwell on the excellent, the praiseworthy, is to dwell on God himself; to dwell is to give attention, and we move in the direction of whatever has our attention.

This is why I needed out of Blacksburg for a time, not to avoid, but to gain perspective, to learn balance. After the funerals for six dead children, a friend of the Bryants offered the family a free vacation to Alaska so they could get out, get away, and make new memories. While on a train through the Alaskan countryside, Joyce felt God whisper within her, "Joyce, if I could make all of this, I can take care of you as well."

The gift of that trip — and God bless whoever gave it — was a step toward healing. In taking the step, the Bryants did not avoid their grief. They carried it with them, I'm sure. But the trip was a necessary move toward perspective and peace.

Five

I am looking for gifts — for balance and perspective. Some years ago (in April, appropriately) I was struck by the thought that every good thing in life is a gift.

Heading home that day, I took the back country roads and was moved, more than usual, by the gift of beauty all around: the soft, gray ceiling of clouds hanging just above the misty blue mountains; a light, persistent rain preparing the earth for the new growth of spring; and rolling fields already ripe with the green of the new season. So much beauty! Even in a world falling farther every day into rebellion against its Creator. This beauty that for a short while can make everything seem okay — surely this is a gift.

Winding through Ellett Valley, I thought of friends who were at that moment in dark places, wrestling with life. And something more certain than hope came over me, and I knew that they were okay, and I was okay, and the universe was okay. And all would be well because the Artist had not abandoned his work. I was all of a sudden very much at peace. And that was a gift.

A few lines from singer Chris Tomlin — ah, the gift of worship — drifted through my mind as I traveled toward home (and home is a gift).

> He wraps Himself in light
> And darkness tries to hide
> And trembles at His voice.[20]

Tremble, indeed, I thought. "The darkness is passing.... The night is nearly over."[21] And that is a gift.

Until the night is over, it is important to look for gifts, for anything lovely or admirable in the world. These are reminders that God is good even when life isn't. Gifts come alongside in our suffering, offering perspective in our pain, balance for our grief. They quietly call out, like whispers on the wind, echoes from a world that was.

We tend to think of grace as a gift offered after the fall, as a response to our sin. But grace is merely any goodness or favor that isn't earned. For Adam and Eve, newly created beings, this was everything. They did nothing to merit existence, so life itself was grace. The pure air they breathed, the beauty around them, the love in their souls for each other and for God — *everything* was a gift.

Mercy followed the fall, but grace has been with us from the beginning.

Long ago the world was wholly good and all of life was a gift from the hand of a loving God. It isn't so anymore. Evil and suffering have marred the earth so that much of what comes to us is not what God intended. If we do not, therefore, search out good in the midst of our pain, if we do not look for the lovely and the admirable and then dwell on the gifts we find, we will be tempted toward despair. We'll lose perspective.

James reminds us in the New Testament that "every good and perfect gift is from above, coming down from the Father of the heavenly lights, who does not change like shifting shadows."[22] He is the same now as then. When I receive his gifts, when I remember to look for them, I taste and see that he is good, even when life around me isn't.

Six

We at Tech received many gifts after April 16. Thousands of them, some big, some small—all precious to us. One gift in particular will stand out forever in my mind.

Two days after the massacre, the pastoral team of my church met to decide how to handle the next two Sunday services. It was a nearly impossible task. What seemed totally inappropriate one day—smiles and laughter and looking ahead—would be absolutely essential for coping the next. The needs of the community changed by the hour. How could we possibly predict the mood of the campus, and of our congregation, two weeks down the road?

We did the only thing we could. We prayed for wisdom, then made our best guess. The first Sunday would be a simple service, honest and raw, with time for a question-and-answer session. For week two we decided to seek outside help. Maybe an event was out of place; a spectacle would be offensive. But was there anyone we could invite who would come quietly, humbly, looking to serve, not to make a splash? Someone who could speak into our tragedy without having been consumed by it, as we were?

"What about Philip Yancey?" I asked.

I'd be lying if I said there wasn't something selfish in the suggestion. If Madeleine L'Engle is my sage, then Philip Yancey is my hero. His writings have moved me past many dry spells in my faith. Undoubtedly, the chance to meet him influenced my recommendation.

I am a reader, a writer, a believer, a doubter. The same with my heroes. Philip Yancey's books routinely ask (and answer) troubling questions, *his* questions, about faith in an invisible God. He writes honestly and with a reporter's curiosity. That authenticity has helped me work through a host of nagging doubts.

And it just made sense to invite him. He has spent his career circling around the universal problem of pain. His works include *Where Is God When It Hurts?* and *Disappointment with God.* Of all the people we considered, Yancey's name rose time and again to the top.

And what a comfort to speak with him on the phone while on my way out the door to a funeral for one of the April 16 victims. Yancey was immediately sensitive to the pastors' concern that the tone of the service be subtle, suited to the needs of the Tech community. As we worked out details for his visit, Yancey again made certain the plan would be a help, not a hindrance. He wanted to bring with him his wife, Janet, and a few friends, including a young woman, Kacey, who was shot in the shoulder at Columbine. "But," he said, "we certainly don't want to impose anything or try to orchestrate something that wouldn't be an act of grace and practical help to your grieving community. If all this seems overwhelming, or somehow wrong, just blow the whistle and it's over."

With servants' hearts, Philip and the company he brought came only to give, not to impose. They insisted on paying for everything and made only one request of us: "Can we have Virginia Tech T-shirts? We'd like to be Hokies too."

Like Jesus, who put on human flesh to become one of us, they too wished to wear our skin, to identify. What a gift to us they were. And a costly gift, at that: Philip was in a neck brace from a serious car accident several weeks earlier, so travel was a challenge. And in addition to his sacrifice, his publisher donated twelve hundred copies of his book *Where Is God When It Hurts?*—one for each person who would attend the Sunday service.

Philip, Janet, and friends arrived midafternoon on a Saturday, and though they were with us for just twenty-four hours, the gift of their presence, of their coming alongside, will remain with me forever. They visited the Hokie stones, saw the tens of thousands of sympathetic expressions spread around the campus. The pain in the eyes of Kacey from Columbine was obvious. She told me, "It's been eight years since the shootings there, and I've only recently begun to feel the anger." Kacey's words made clear for me how permanent is the change April has brought to our community, how enduring will be its effects. The stones may go away, but the impression they've left will not.

The next morning, during the service in the Virginia Tech student center, Philip Yancey offered no answers, only solace.

Why this campus rather than Virginia Commonwealth or William and Mary? Why these thirty-three people? I cannot tell you, and I encourage you to resist anyone who offers a confident answer. God himself did not answer Job, nor did Jesus answer "why" questions. We have hints, but no one knows the full answer. What we do know, with full confidence, is how God feels. We know how God looks on the campus of Virginia Tech right now because God has a face....

The Jews, schooled in the Old Testament, had a saying: "Where Messiah is, there is no misery." After Jesus, you could change that saying to "Where misery is, there is the Messiah." "Blessed are the poor," Jesus said, "and those who hunger and thirst, and those who mourn, and those who are persecuted." Jesus voluntarily embraced every one of these hurts.

So where is God when it hurts? We know where God is because he came to earth and showed us his face.[23]

And in this much-needed reminder, I experienced the goodness of that God-with-a-face.

Pain blurs our vision, makes us lose sight of truths that would otherwise seem obvious. In suffering, I am prone to forget God has a name, that he is not an abstraction, not simply an energy floating around somewhere in or out of the universe. He is a Person. His name is Jesus. And what Jesus is, God is. Or, as Scripture says, Jesus is the "exact representation"[24] of God's being.

In his book *Reaching for the Invisible God*, Yancey writes:

I cannot learn from Jesus why bad things occur — why an avalanche or flood decimates one town and not its neighbor, why leukemia strikes one child and not another — but I can surely learn how God feels about such tragedies. I simply look at how Jesus responds to the sisters of his good friend Lazarus, to a widow who has just lost her son, or a leprosy victim banned outside the town gates. Jesus gives God a face, and that face is streaked with tears.[25]

It sounds simple enough, till grief takes the obvious and obscures it. Then we need the gift of reminders. Philip Yancey reminded me that my God has a name, that I don't have to wonder whether Jesus cares that I'm sad. I can know. "Where misery is, there is the Messiah."

When the time came, I wished everyone a safe trip back to Colorado and told them I looked forward to visiting their state in the summer.

"Oh, you're coming out to Colorado? What part?" Janet asked.

"Estes Park, to speak at a conference. I can't wait. I've always wanted to see the Rockies."

"Estes Park is not far from us," Janet said. "Let us know when you'll be there."

I've heard it said that when God wished to give his greatest gift, that of himself, he wrapped it in human flesh. He still gives this way, his presence mysteriously clothed in dust that is returning to dust. Philip and Janet and the friends they brought with them became to us the skin of Christ, a tangible reminder that God was still good, and very much with us, even in our tears and confusion.

Just before slipping out the door for the airport, Janet turned and said again, "I mean it—let us know when you'll be in Colorado."

Some moments in life are so wondrous they defy description. Your first time seeing the ocean, or holding your newborn child in your arms — nothing can prepare you for that feeling, and how would you ever describe it? You'd try but would finally conclude, "No, that's not quite it. I don't know how to say it. I can't find the words." This is me through Colorado. I am beyond the limits of language.

There is a point on I-70, heading west out of Denver, coming out of a curve, when you suddenly see them; they flash into view as if God spoke them into being that very instant: the majestic snow-capped Rockies. "They appear out of nowhere," a friend warned, "and the sight will steal your breath."

Nothing prepares. The exhilaration is like that of reaching the height of a symphony. Everything — the blackness of April, Dad's fall in May, all the sadness since — everything has built toward this moment, this gift of beauty. I am glad I did not see the Rockies before this summer. They would have inspired, of course. But never before have I had such a thirst for them.

A phrase from Romans comes to mind, out of nowhere as well, as if it too were just now spoken into being. *At just the right time . . .*

"At just the right time . . . Christ died for the ungodly"[26] and gave us the gift of life. He is like this with his gifts, I guess. He knows exactly when they are needed, knew just when to give the Rockies.

Prompted by the glory, my eyes fill, and the snowcaps melt into a watery blur. Four times between the airport and the Yanceys' home, I tear up. I am not typically a crier; this is highly unusual.

But then, what is normal anymore? Likely I will always look back on this year as utterly surreal. How should I comprehend a mass murder in my backyard, the worst shooting in modern U.S. history? Meeting my hero in the same month? Getting my first look at the Rockies? Things unimaginable, indescribable, are now the norm. Nothing is "usual" about this year, and it calls for tears. Words alone are not enough.

Every moment is apt to feel wondrous this summer. The so-called simple things of life are hardly simple anymore. They are brimming with glory and goodness.

As I said, Philip Yancey and I first spoke by phone as I was on my way out the door to the funeral for Caitlin Hammaren, one of the victims of the Tech massacre. After that service, and in the days that followed as I read the biographies of each of the dead, a strong desire grew within me to really live and not waste time.

"What happened in Blacksburg on April 16," Yancey said to our church two weeks after the tragedy, "demonstrates beyond all doubt that your life—the decisions you make, the kind of person you are—matters *now*. There are twenty-eight students and five faculty members who have no future in this world."[27]

April was not the first time I have felt this. I once made a goal to live an entire year as if it were my last on earth. I'd awake each morning to the quote "Living this year like it's my last." Last time to watch this movie, or see this friend, or drink eggnog at Christmas, or drive through Craig County when the leaves turn in autumn. Last chance to do all the things I had put off for "another time."

The point was to see how life would be different if I truly, deep down, believed the obvious, that existence here could be over any minute. What I found is that nothing much changed about the big decisions. I had no desire to quit my job and be a missionary to Africa, or run around finding long-lost friends so I could tell them I love them one last time. What changed was my enjoyment of the simple. Craig County in autumn was that much more splendid. Eggnog never tasted so good. Nothing was more perfect than lingering long by a dying campfire with cherished friends. Every moment, the simple as much as the grand, mattered. *Now* mattered.

My visit with the Yanceys, at their home in Colorado, is a time of constant *now*. Each instant is important, something to be truly lived. I wind through a canyon on my way to their home on a hill. The big matters: that I'm spending an evening with the Yanceys. But equally so does the small. That I'm winding through a canyon, any canyon at all in the world, is simple yet profound.

As I arrive at their house, it is Philip first, then Janet, who is out the door to meet me.

"Hey, you found us," Philip says. He is out of his neck brace.

"What do you think of Colorado so far?" asks Janet.

"It's beautiful, everything I imagined it would be."

"Good!" Janet says. "Come on inside."

Philip leads me and my luggage downstairs to the room where I will sleep tonight. On the way, we pass his office and the desk where he writes.

"Take your time getting settled in," Philip says, "then come upstairs, and I'll show you the view from the deck. You'll love it."

I set my bags down, then stare a few moments into the office. Rows of books rest on shelves, and parallel to them sits the desk where Yancey writes. And next to it a window. He has written about this view in one of his books: "Through my office window I now look upon ... the glint of snow off 14,000-foot mountains."[28] I experience a sudden delight at the realization I am staring at the same sight.

Upstairs, Janet begins work on dinner. "Matt, have you ever had ostrich burgers?"

Indeed, I have not. Do grocery stores in Virginia even stock ostrich? Little things like this — that Colorado carries ostrich at the meat counter — are what I love about the new world I'm in. Out on the deck, Philip introduces me to the names of this new world: evergreen, ponderosa pine, aspen trees.

"In the morning," Philip says, "we'll take you for a walk through the woods behind the house. The wildflowers this year are profuse thanks to good snows in the winter."

As the burgers sizzle on the grill, Philip, Janet, and I catch up on life since our meeting a little more than a month earlier. They want to know how the students are doing. "It's hard to tell now that school is out," I say. "We'll hear from some of them this summer, but most we won't know about till they return in the fall."

I wonder and worry about them too, how they're doing back home. Grief and trauma counselors warned us that for some students, signs of post-traumatic stress would not show up for weeks, maybe months after April 16, and that the hardest part for many would be going home. Separated from friends who shared the experience, students would be suddenly immersed in communities far from Tech that had viewed the events of April as spectators, all wanting to know "What was it like?" and "How are you doing?"

"Everywhere they go, they're going to be asked about it," Philip says. "That will be hard."

And it is hard not knowing whom I should be concerned about, whose wound is hidden but festering. I talked to a student only a couple of weeks ago who felt ashamed she was still struggling with the massacre when everyone else seemed to have moved on. First, I assured her everyone had *not* moved on, that I'd had more than a few similar conversations with other students who felt the same as she. Second, I encouraged her to take her time with the grief and the anger: "Thirty-two people — friends, classmates, mentors — were slain on our campus," I said. "That's not something people get over in a few weeks, nor should they. Take your time, and move forward at a pace that seems good to you. But by no means should you feel ashamed."

How many more like her are sitting at home now, hiding, needlessly embarrassed to be still affected?

Dinner is ready. We eat out on the deck. Philip and Janet graciously give me the seat facing the snowcapped peaks. Every bite of food tonight is somehow more than it might otherwise be. The joy I receive is like that of tasting food for the first time. There is wonder in every mouthful. Ever since April I've noticed this heightening of my senses. I feel everything acutely. The bad seems especially terrible. The good, inexpressibly better.

After dinner, Philip offers a prayer of thanks for our meal and asks for healing after the spring: "Continue to be with Matt as he has been affected by the shootings in ways he may not even yet be aware."

And as Philip prays, I privately thank God for this time that is both big and small, when every instant matters, and even the simple is profound. I am thankful for the chance to get out and get away, for the Yanceys' offer of balance and perspective. Perhaps the world is awful, but it is beautiful as well, and I am grateful for the blessing of being here.

Eight

Grateful forever, and to the point of guilt. Why have these gifts come to me? And I *am* mindful they are given: the apostle Paul warned the Corinthians against assuming the goodness of God came by their own doing, or simply happened upon them. "What do you have that God hasn't given you?" he asked. "And if everything you have is from God, why boast as though it were not a gift?"[29]

The Yanceys have turned in for the night, and I lie here in a bed downstairs, awake with wonder, and I know with every atom of my being that none of this is by chance. The goodness of God has led me here.

Why is it that when evil occurs, all appears random, chaotic? We cannot work it out or find a purpose in it. But let a little good come our way and at once all seems ordained. Perhaps even *preordained*, as if this were the plan all along. Can we have it both ways?

Maybe so. Perhaps goodness is so much the natural fiber of the world—at least the world as God intended it—that providence is written into the fabric of every gift that comes to us. We say, "Of course. It was obviously meant to be. This is the work of God in my life." Evil, by contrast, is an intrusion into God's design, a disruption, and so appears anarchic, disordered, meaningless.

I had this same thought after 9/11. For hours I sat in front of the TV with the rest of the world, watching the towers fall, trying to comprehend the depth of darkness required for such a thing. And I could not. I simply could not get my mind around it. The thought finally came to me that perhaps I am not supposed to understand. That something would be wrong with me if I could give an answer to the why of all this. Buildings and bodies cascading to the ground as crumpled debris from a hundred stories up — it's not in the original DNA of the world, or of the people the Designer made. We stare at our screens and cannot turn away because we have not the ability to process the horror. We stand there dumbfounded, trying to understand the inexplicable. We were not meant to.

Goodness and evil are such total opposites, one cannot relate to the other. The poetic apostle John wrote, "The Light shines in the darkness, and the darkness did not comprehend it."[30] So evil is out of place, and goodness, when it comes to us, is a gift. And we know it.

But why me? Why do I receive gifts? Why am I given an evening with a hero while Matt La Porte takes a bullet? (Does he have a headstone yet? Has the ground settled over his grave?)

From the many stories published in April, I know that Matt was a quiet student, "secretly brilliant,"[31] with a "beautiful sense of humor."[32] Friends in high school nicknamed him "Turtle"[33] for an interest he held in the hard-shelled creatures.[34] He "loved art and music and planned to join the Air Force after college."[35]

And he loved his family. In his high school senior oration at Carson Long Military Institute, Matt credited his parents for their support of him: "You've been relentless and persistent, putting your all into me. I love you. And Dad, I hope that I've become a man in your eyes, and that whatever I do in life, you are proud of me."[36]

Every time I read this, I trip over the words "whatever I do in life," knowing that when he wrote them, Matt had less than two years left in the world. And he was, according to one mentor, "desperate to make a difference."[37]

Yet here I am, and not Matt, and it isn't fair, and I don't know how to work it out. How, even, should I share with friends my joy at being here? It feels wrong. If I boast about a night with the Yanceys, they know, as I know, that I met them at the expense of thirty-three lives. How would my boasting sound to the La Porte family? Would my joy be an offense to them?

I suppose it will be this way for a while, feeling bad about feeing good. Happiness laced with guilt. That delicate dance after tragedy, wondering when it's okay to laugh again. I bet Derek O'Dell felt the same guilt, wondering why he is here and not another. But as he observed, if my being here isn't from God, then I have "no logical explanation" for it.

And I'd go mad if I had no God to thank for all this, for peaches and ice cream and coffee with the Yanceys after dinner tonight; for conversation with Philip about our favorite authors; for tales of the "14-ers" he and Janet have climbed. ("14-ers," I learn, is a nickname for the 14,000-foot peaks of Colorado.)

I do not know why I am here, and not Matt, or any one of the thirty-two others. But I know I cannot forever feel bad about feeling good. And as unfair as it may be — and it does seem terribly so — I cannot reject these blessings or pretend they came by my own cunning. Better, I guess, to accept these gifts as a child would — with eager delight — and experience the goodness of God in them.

In the morning, after a breakfast of omelets on the deck, and with the little time we have left before I leave for Estes Park, the Yanceys and I go walking through the woods around their home, spying wildflowers. Janet knows them all, names each one as we pass by: harebells, Indian paintbrush (which so intrigues me that I stop to snap a picture), and the peculiarly named toadflax.

"And there's columbine over there," Janet says.

"Columbine is a flower?" I ask.

"It's the *state* flower," she answers.

I had no idea. As with the sweet-scented candles by the Hokie stones back home, here too is irony, that the name of a thing so graceful and elegant should be forever tainted by its association with evil. How many of us are awake enough to creation to know that columbine was a flower before it was a tragedy?

By this I am reminded why Philip, and now Janet as well, is a hero. They maintain balance, give attention to beauty, despite living in reality. They have not hidden themselves from the heavy sadness of the world. Rather, they have immersed themselves in it. Janet is a hospice chaplain; she deals in death's sting. Philip once lost three close friends in the same year. He hangs out in cancer support groups and AA meetings with friends, listens long and responds honestly to their painful, troublesome doubts. Growing up, Philip endured a damaging relationship with a graceless church, nearly leaving the faith in his disappointment. Now he spends his life searching out answers to tough spiritual questions many of us fear asking.

Philip and Janet know difficulty. They embrace the world as it is yet maintain perspective. They see good as well as bad, take the time and make the effort to learn the names of wildflowers, which much of the world breezes past in its crazed rush and hurry.

Back at the house, it's time to leave. I say good-bye to Janet, thanking her for my visit.

"Come stay with us again," she says, "when you can stay longer."

Philip leads me out to I-70 by a route that takes us past Red Rocks Park. Massive slabs of rust-colored sandstone rise from the earth at a 45-degree tilt, as if one day the crust of the planet shifted and sank, half buried.

This is not far from what geologists believe happened. I've read that here once stood the Ancestral Rocky Mountains, of which these slabs are all that remain. Scientists think those mountains eroded over millions of years, hardened, and slowly reddened from iron in the water passing through the rocks. Buried for eons, the rusty rocks rose again when the present-day Rocky Mountains surfaced.[38]

What awful quaking forced their rise from the earth at such a slant? It must have been a horror to witness, that cataclysmic crashing and splitting and bursting forth, the site of which is now, by irony, a peaceful park for tourists.

Another icon: those rocks are beauty born out of violence. Years from now, once the dust has settled, what will people see in us? Can beauty grow from the soil of this spring? Can we become as lovely?

Yancey and I pull over and hop out for a final good-bye.

"Well, I guess this is it. Come see us again," Philip says, echoing his wife.

"I'd like that."

Ten

Estes Park must be a pseudonym for Eden, a rose by some other name. Here is the closest thing I've seen to how I imagine the lost world might have appeared. I am catching echoes by the minute. Never was the sky bluer. Never has the sun's warmth so invigorated. And the snowcapped peaks: I stare at them in awe. It's a struggle to look at anything else, even to watch where I'm walking. I trip all over Eden.

And as with the coast, so with the mountains: I have come here to teach, but more so to learn, to sit in silence and let creation do its healing work. I want to give attention to wonder, to choose balance. I am embracing the gift of the Rockies, however unfairly it has come to me.

The schedule for the week is wonderfully relaxed. By day, college students attending this leadership conference work various jobs around the YMCA here. Main sessions, where I speak, are in the evenings after dinner, so I have the whole day to myself. Other than a little last-minute prep for my teachings, I am free and on my own.

Some days I stake out a spot on the grand, wood-planked porch of the log YMCA administration building, perfectly situated with a view of the mountains. From here I watch the sun at day's end slip beneath the horizon, casting the underbellies of clouds in various shades of pink and purple, the subtleties of which I've never seen before. It is all, in L'Engle's words, "achingly beautiful."[39]

Other days I go for a hike. Rocky Mountain National Park is just up the road. One evening, after a teaching, Chris, a student intern with the leadership program, offers to take me up Emerald Mountain. "You can get a great view of the snowcaps from there," Chris says. We set out the next morning from a trailhead at the edge of the Y. The climb is steep, the pace brisk. Thankfully, though, it's a short hike; my lungs are still adapting to Colorado's thin, dry air.

The view from the top is intoxicating, worth all the panting and gasping to get there: aspen and evergreen at my feet; brilliant blue hanging overhead; and in between, the grassy fields, at first sloping gently upward, then shooting straight into the air in a sudden, rocky eruption.

I am eye-level with the peaks. From this angle, the jagged ridge resembles the sharp teeth of a dog's jaw. Like a panoramic dental X-ray, giant black molars jut from the gum of the earth, with snow for decay caked in the crevices. Seen from here, the Rockies are a somewhat playful sight, less daunting than from below, more simply intriguing than fearsome. Standing on tiptoe I am taller than they. *I am the "14-er."*

It's all an illusion, of course. I am barely nine thousand feet above the sea. The snowcaps before me are thousands of feet higher. The distance from here to there gives me a false sense of stature.

There is, however, nothing false about the childish wonder I feel standing here. Chris and I make seats out of two adjacent rocks, sit, and face the mountains, both catching echoes of the world that was. *If this is what remains, how majestic must the real thing have been. And how good its Designer.*

———

Everyone gathers at mealtimes into a large dining hall. The students and staff are hesitant to mention April 16, but I can tell they wish to talk about it, knowing, as they do, where I'm from. I can see it in the way they look at me from across the table. It's in their eyes. They are wondering what is appropriate, judging whether they should ask, "What was it like?"

This curiosity strikes me as both natural and good. We are all understandably interested in the human situation, and it encourages me that these students want to speak of the real world rather than run from it. They realize it could have been their school, their church, their friends. That it might be someday. They want to know how they would respond.

Eventually someone musters the courage to ask, albeit sheepishly, about my experience. I smile and engage, doing my best to set folks at ease. "You can ask anything you like," I say, stealing a line from Derek O'Dell. "I don't mind talking about it."

Mostly the questions are familiar—What was it like? What were you feeling?—the same questions I asked Derek and the Bryants. This time, however, I'm the one answering.

One student wonders, "Were you scared?"

"No," I say. "Cho was dead before I knew anything had happened."

"Where were you during the shootings?" another asks. "Were you near?"

"I was sitting in Starbucks, about a ten-minute walk from Norris

Hall. No one in Starbucks had any idea what was happening nearby. It was like any other morning, except for how cold it was for mid-April. I remember walking outside the coffee shop a little after ten o'clock, twenty minutes or so after the massacre, and hearing a voice from a distant loudspeaker. My only thought was that maybe they were testing the sound system at the football stadium. It wasn't until I got home and turned on the TV that I realized something was very wrong."

"What were you thinking when you heard the news?"

"Well," I respond, "the details were slow in coming. It was hours before we knew how bad the situation was. At first, the news outlets reported one death in a dormitory on campus. Then two dead, with several injuries. Some of the stations began reporting a second incident in an academic building. Eight people dead. I remember feeling a sense of dread once the death toll jumped from eight to over twenty. At that point, you knew this was not a one-or two-day story on the news. This was going to change everything."

"How did your church respond?"

"We got our staff and small group leaders together that afternoon, made sure they were okay, and talked through what to do. We figured that by evening names would be coming in, and students would probably just want to be together, so we planned a prayer vigil for that night. Then the reporters started calling—CNN, NPR, and the like—all wanting interviews, wanting to know why we thought God would let this happen, if this had shaken our faith at all."

"Were the media awful?" asks one of the staff at the Y.

"Actually," I say, "a lot of us thought the media handled themselves well. I don't recall much anger from the students directed at the hundreds of news outlets. We understood they had a job to do, and with a few exceptions, the reporters carried themselves pretty well, I think. I'm sure some people would disagree—people who had a camera shoved in their face while they were trying to grieve. A number of media outlets came to our first service after the massacre. As they arrived, we gave them guidelines we wanted them to follow before, during, and after the service. Their cameras had to remain stationary the whole time, no moving around. And they could only interview students whose permission we'd obtained in advance. I suppose legally they didn't have to do anything we asked, but they followed our suggestions to the letter. So no one felt violated by the presence of the reporters. The media were there. They got their story. But they were discreet. And honestly, we wanted the media at our service, watching people worship in spite of pain. We didn't want the last thing the world saw to be Cho aiming his gun at a camera."

"What did the reporters ask?"

"Mostly they wanted to know what questions our church was asking and how we were answering them. Thing is, no one was asking questions, at least not at first. Everyone was just in shock and very sad. The hard questions didn't come till later. That first night, and then again many times over the next few weeks, we reminded our church how much weight words carry in a moment like that, when the whole world is listening. We asked them to watch what they said, to not respond out of hate or anger or bitterness, and not to participate if they heard others doing so. We just didn't want our church adding more grief to an already painful situation, so the other pastors and I kept quoting Romans 12:21: 'Do not be overcome by evil, but overcome evil with good.' We kept saying it till we began hearing others saying it, till we were sure the message had got across."

As the questions continue, and the answers follow, something akin to joy warms me. Remembering that week, offering details about it, is strangely therapeutic. The more I reflect on that time, the more certain I am that we did very much experience God as good. It didn't *feel* good, of course, and nothing could ever make what happened good. But I can see a trail of grace running through the many long days that followed the tragedy. How many interviews did we endure? How many answers were we compelled to give on the spot, no time to think or formulate a clever response? Yet I cannot remember any significant stumbles. Might this not have been the goodness of God, the gift of his presence, carrying us along? Again, it did not *feel* good, but maybe it will be this way sometimes. Perhaps to experience is not always to feel.

"Thanks for talking with us," someone says at the end of the meal, after exhausting all the questions.

It is a thoroughly odd sensation to be so far from home, fifteen hundred miles from such a little place as Blacksburg, and to have everyone around asking about it, craving a firsthand account of the happenings there. Here are the people who saw us kneel beside the stones. We knew they were "out there," watching. Now I am "out here" with them. I see their faces, can look into the eyes that watched us drying ours. And I know that in compassion, they were drying theirs too. They were weeping alongside us.

John, the director of this leadership program, and also a pastor, tells me how his church in Missouri responded to April 16. Thirty-three members of his congregation, each carrying a poster with the name and age of one of our dead, slowly marched to the front during their service so that everyone could see and sense the enormity of loss. His church then prayed for us, imagining themselves in our shoes.

No wonder they now ask about my experience. Though many miles removed, they shared it. And likewise, they share its lingering questions. I sense in these students and staff more than morbid musing. People are asking, same as I am asking—same as I asked Derek and the Bryant family: Is it okay? Is the world all right? Is God still good when life isn't?

Now that it's my turn to speak, I want to answer, "No. And yes." No, the world is not all right. How could it be? But yes, God is good. Maybe I can't always feel it, but I'm beginning to taste and see.

Eleven

Two things one learns quickly in Colorado: the air is thin and the sun, severe. I head into town to buy sunscreen, stopping at a Safeway grocery store.

Turns out there is nothing safe about it. The cashier reaches to hand me my receipt and notices the Virginia Tech shirt I made the mistake of wearing. "Virginia Tech," he says. "Your school is infamous now."

There is instant fire in my chest and in my eyes, and the man knows it. He backpedals quickly: "... which ... is ... unfortunate ... you guys sure have a great football team ... shame you gotta be known for this...."

Snatching my receipt and my sunscreen, I make for the door to keep from saying something rash. Once outside, I fight the urge to go back in and yell at the man. *My home is not infamous—it is wonderful and you will respect it!*

Why this sudden rage? The man obviously didn't mean what he

said to sound so bad. April is a wound beginning to heal, yet still tender. I forget it for moments, till I hit it on something. Or someone.

And sadly, the man is right. We *are* now known for tragedy, and yelling will not change that. Anger will only make it worse. Isn't this what I told my church—overcome evil with good? But can anything ever overcome this? Can anything replace Cho as the first thought people have about my home? It'll be years before we know.

—

Back at my room in Estes Park, I find pictures from inside the second floor of Norris Hall all over news websites. Virginia Tech has opened the building to media for the first time since April. I stare at a silent slideshow, gawking as one might while slowly driving past a traffic accident.

I feel in my gut a gaping emptiness, a vacuum that mirrors the images of vacant classrooms. My eyes look deep into whitewashed walls and drown in the watery, freshly waxed floors. There are no chairs, no desks, no signs of any life, as if all were sucked from the place by evil itself.

The school did well cleaning up the mess. Too well, perhaps. Norris looks new: new paint on walls, new doors hung from their hinges, and newly buffed floors reflecting fluorescent lights. It is all too pure, too clean. *What are you hiding, Norris? Are you hoping we'll forget?*

As if we ever could.

Is there anyplace I could go—anyplace in the world—beyond the reach of Norris Hall, where I would not wear a scarlet VT? Could I find a corner of the globe where I wouldn't have to think twice when reaching for a Tech T-shirt? Where I could truly be away, and alone, for even a little while?

Twelve

Shortly after the scene in Safeway, Laura Ruth, a friend back home who is a flight attendant, calls to offer me a free trip to Japan. I jump at the chance despite more guilt: *I didn't lose six children or watch my classmates die. Why should I . . . ?*

But why not? *Matt, the gift is offered. Receive it as a child would.*

And who knew thirteen hours could pass so quickly? With shades down to allow passengers sleep, I soon forget I'm in the air, and before long, we're landing. When leaving the States, I wondered whether I'd be homesick, this being the farthest from home I'd ever strayed. But as we taxi toward the terminal in Narita, Japan, all I can think is how small the world now seems. It took only hours to reach the other side. I think of the men who traveled to the moon during the *Apollo* days. Were they homesick watching earthrise? Or did they say, "It's just four days away"?

It is not the things I expected that surprise me about Japan. The people have a darker skin tone, yes; they speak a language foreign to me. But having anticipated these differences, I hardly notice them at all. And much about this place is oddly similar to home. Sky is still sky, water still water, even on the other side of the world. The countryside and foothills here are not unlike those of southwest Virginia. Distant, it would seem, does not mean different.

It is other, smaller, completely unexpected things that catch me off guard. I cannot stop commenting on how quiet the airport is in Narita. Same number of people as in an American airport of comparable size, yet not half as loud. Even the streets of Tokyo, the nation's largest city, are hushed by U.S. standards. Horn-honking is a last resort rather than a first response; cars whiz by rather than roar. And clean: the sidewalks and alleys of all but a few areas are immaculate. I see no public trash cans anywhere we go, yet the country is swept of any litter. Roads appear freshly and evenly paved, or barely used, as in an amusement park.

I am in Wonderland here. I am over the rainbow, or through the wardrobe, here in the Land of the Rising Sun. Everywhere I turn, and like a small child, I am thrilled by the sight and sound of little things never before experienced. A strange and foreign birdcall from a tree overhanging the street steals my attention. Though it is likely the scratch and caw of a common crow, I am utterly fascinated by this "something new." *Thirty years old and still a kid, still discovering new things.*

Perhaps Japan's greatest draw for me is simply that it isn't home. From the Bryants I learned the blessing of "away." Their Alaskan voyage after tragedy was not escape or denial. It was a temporary but necessary reprieve from a place that would never be the same. No one here knows my name or where I live. There is not the least chance anyone will ask about Cho. How desperately I need this, to see there is a world outside my home, untouched by April and everything after.

Two days in the old imperial Kyoto assures me of this. With a population of 1.5 million, Kyoto is, at first glance, as dense and claustrophobic as any city in the world, modern and newly constructed. But head for the mountains, the foothills at the edge of town, slip just beneath the tree line, and you step back in time hundreds of years to a lost world of secluded temples and shrines and Zen gardens. The bustling of the city dissolves, as if banished from these hills by a powerful, ancient serenity that still lingers in this place.

Casually, unhurriedly, I stroll through the gardens under the cool of shade along pebbled paths. All is silent except nature's sounds. Water trickles over rocks jutting from the mountainside. Japanese maple leaves rustle from a slight breeze. A nearby pond gurgles with fish surfacing for a snack, then ducking under again. I kneel by the water's edge and run my hand through a soft carpet of dew-drenched moss, bright green like that of new spring, covering the ground.

I cannot recall the last time I was this quiet or this much at rest, nothing to say, no one to save. I have not come for a conference, and my cell phone will not work. The heaviest weight of April, the sense that the whole world was listening to (and judging Jesus by) our words, falls away. Here, even if I were to speak, no one would understand the language. Not only are answers not expected of me in this place, but I could not give them if they were. Here, all is peace, and I feel a special kinship with my oldest ancestors; they too walked with God through a garden by the cool of day.

Jesus left us this example, which I follow through Kyoto's hills: retreating to the mountains for silence and solitude. The gospel of Matthew tells us that Jesus once spent a whole night alone on a hill in prayer to God. Especially intriguing to me — and this summer, it makes total sense — is that Jesus, after learning of the death of his cousin, John the Baptist, responded to grief by withdrawing "to a solitary place."[40] His need was not for answers, but for God himself. And so intense was the desire for communion, for connection with the goodness of his Father, that he slipped away from the crowds to be alone in the quiet. The reason for doing this, says author Richard Foster, is "not in order to be away from people but in order to hear the divine Whisper better."[41]

"Without silence," Foster says, "there is no solitude."[42] And we need these times of aloneness, moments away to hear the Whisper and to dwell on something other than our broken selves. But it is a choice to make the time. There is so much need at every turn, so much calling out for our attention, that it will take a determined restructuring of our lives to slow down, get away, and simply rest. And we'll have to trust that this resting is not wasted time, that it is actually life-giving and possibly the surest way of avoiding eventual despair. If we do not make a habit of sitting in silence, listening for the whisper of a good God, we will never hear it at all. And we will be left with a half-truth, a world of only deathly sting. This is not the full picture. The world is bad, but it is good, what author Annie Dillard calls "a frayed and beautiful land";[43] it is full of echoes of that once-untainted world. But echoes must be caught.

Thirteen

These moments of respite are gifts indeed, but they are easily interrupted. Not far from the peaceful gardens and the ancient temples and shrines sits a small cemetery on a hill. Beauty all around me, yet I stumble into death, reminded that the curse has reached these parts as well. Nowhere on earth is free of it. Not my precious home. Not the other side of the world.

Even more so than we Americans, the Japanese pack their people in, gravestones crammed together into a sort of village for the dead. Most of the markers are tall and thin, reaching up instead of out, to conserve a little room. I've read that in some cultures short on space, the bereaved bury their loved ones standing up. Here they cremate, storing the remains of many relatives in a small crypt beneath a cramped family plot. It is a matter of efficiency and foresight. Japan is an island only so big; posterity will have to live somewhere.

What will they do in a few hundred years when the dead so vastly exceed the living? (I hear it's already a challenge — nearly impossible—to hold a funeral in Tokyo.) Will the whole country be a grave? Will they have to outlaw cemeteries? Bury a friend, then build a home over top?

And what of us in America? We have more room (for now), but we are no less likely to be covered and forgotten.

I think of another cemetery on a hill, this one back home, thousands of miles from here, in Virginia. I visited there once after reading about it online. The easiest way to it is hardly easy at all, a terribly steep forty-five-minute hike up Sinking Creek Mountain. The trailhead sits obscured, off a back road that is itself a branch off another back road. If you can find the trail at all, and if you make it to the end, you enter a hollow, in which sits the rotted ruins of an old log home, eerily vacant, abandoned. Here the Sarver family once lived. The first-floor walls are weak but holding up; the second story gave way years ago, collapsing in on the lower level. Two sturdy stone chimneys still reach toward the sky. A third fell away from the house when the roof caved in.

A hundred yards from the ruins, up an embankment and perched on a knoll, sits a tiny cemetery, once encircled by now-fallen rusted barbed wire. No trace of any trail leads from the Sarvers' home to their graves, and no marker points the way. David Cheslow, once the caretaker for the trail to the old home, told me about the cemetery and how to find it: "You go straight up the hill ahead and just a bit off to the right. You are looking for four cedar trees in a row. These mark the heads of four graves. The place is full of flowers, which makes it easier to spot in spring."

I went, instead, in November, just after the leaves had fallen, which left the place even more concealed. From the foot of the knoll, I spied the blotch of cedar green on top and thought this had to be it. I couldn't be sure, though, till I was right on the graves—only one of the cedar trees was still living, and the barbed wire hid beneath the browned, dead leaves. Drawing close, I saw the only sure sign, thin slabs of weathered stone rising from the duff. Who were these forgotten souls, covered now by dirt and autumn leaves? Why did they make their home here, tucked away in the Virginia hills?

Little is known of the family. David Cheslow tells me that Henry Sarver immigrated from Germany in the 1800s, where his last name was Serber. Henry served in the Confederate Army during the Civil War and married his sweetheart Sara, and the two made their living as apple and chestnut farmers on Sinking Creek Mountain. They had three daughters, all oddly named Mary, and that's about it. That's all anyone knows, except that the farmhouse was abandoned in the 1930s when a blight killed the chestnut trees.

How do you like that? Your whole family history shrunk to a paragraph. Your three score and ten in three or four lines. Are we so easily reduced? So quickly forgotten? Less than a century since they lived, and who remembers them? I bet not ten people a year pass by their graves.

On my way back down the mountain, I paused by the ruins of their old house. In a sort of hushed reverence, I stood listening as if for echoes of the Sarvers in life. Careful to avoid the exposed, rusted nails in the sagging beams, I stepped inside the dilapidated home, into what I assume was once the kitchen. I closed my eyes, ran my fingers down the rough stones of the fireplace, tried to imagine Sara at the hearth, preparing supper for her family.

When living, while stirring a pot for dinner, did Sara Sarver ever think, "One day I'll be buried on that knoll over there. The wood of my home will rot and give way, and a stranger will stand in the ruins of this house once warmed by love and fire. And hardly anyone in the world will remember I was here. Hardly anyone will care"?

I care. We all should. The Sarvers' story is ours as well. A couple generations from now, who will grieve for us? Will anyone remember we were here? Could you tell me the name of your great-grandfather's dad? Even one important fact about his life (which doubtless seemed so very important to him)?

The writer of Ecclesiastes may have been morbid, but at least he was honest:

> *There is no remembrance of people of old,*
> *and even those who are yet to come*
> *will not be remembered*
> *by those who follow them.*[44]

So balance works both ways. I cannot think only of the curse, nor can I ever quite forget it. It is at home on a hill in Virginia; it is here on a hill in Japan. It is in any and every place I go. The lovely and the admirable give perspective for my pain, but not a final cure. At the end of the day, dead is still dead, no matter how great the beauty one has seen.

Poor suffering Job in his grief cried out, "If someone dies, will they live again?"[45]

It'll take more than echoes to accomplish that.

Fourteen

Not two weeks after returning to the States, I awake to the headline "Earthquake Rocks Japan: Powerful Quake Kills 5, Injures over 500."[46] I watch the reports and think, *I was just there*. I feel as though I'm dodging death everywhere I go. Must I now keep an eye on nature too?

The slightest digging reveals that Japan is among our planet's most earthquake-prone countries, resting on four tectonic plates.[47] In 1995 a 7.3 quake killed 6,400 in the city of Kobe. The Great Kanto Earthquake of 1923 wiped out more than 100,000.[48]

What is going on here? Is creation all I've made it out to be? "Or," as Annie Dillard asks, "is beauty itself an intricately fashioned lure, the cruelest hoax of all?"[49]

Following a long discourse on waves, on how much she loves them, Dillard writes, killing her own joy and mine, "It took only a few typhoon waves to drown 138,000 Bangladeshi on April 30, 1991."[50]

"Look to the sea," I've said. What would the Bangladeshi think if they did?

Or the Indonesians? The Indian Ocean swallowed more than 200,000 of them in 2004. The death toll from that December's tsunami remains unfathomable.

> Indonesia: 230,261
> Sri Lanka: 30,957
> India: 16,413
> Thailand: 5,390
> Maldives: 82
> Malaysia: 68
> Burma: 61
> Bangladesh: 2
> Somalia: 298
> Tanzania: 10
> Kenya: 1
> Total: 283,543[51]

And more than a million and a half people were displaced from their homes.[52]

The sea is certainly double-tongued. To the Israelites, it spoke goodness: "The waters were divided, and the Israelites went through the sea on dry ground."[53] And to the Egyptians? "The LORD swept them into the sea."[54]

At least the Egyptians had it coming; they hunted the Israelites, despite God's having said to let them go. The Bangladeshi and the Indonesians simply woke one morning and drowned.

So much for nature's balm.

The apostle Paul says that in the beginning, along with man, the creation fell.

Against its will, all creation was subjected to God's curse. But with eager hope, the creation looks forward to the day when it will join God's children in glorious freedom from death and decay. For we know that all creation has been groaning as in the pains of childbirth right up to the present time.[55]

So nature, for all its glory, is something less than it once was. Like the people who inhabit it, the natural world is a mix of beauty and horror. It too is twisted, groaning with us, sharing in our decay.

Annie Dillard recognized this and divided her Pulitzer prize-winning theodicy, *Pilgrim at Tinker Creek*, into two parts, the positive and the negative. With a touch of humor and poetic prose, she writes:

Ten percent of all the world's species are parasitic insects. It is hard to believe. What if you were an inventor, and you made ten percent of your inventions in such a way that they could only work by harassing, disfiguring, or totally destroying the other ninety-percent?

… It is the thorn in the flesh of the world, another sign, if any be needed, that the world is actual and fringed, pierced here and there, and through and through, with the toothed conditions of time and the mysterious, coiled spring of death.[56]

Or to say it more simply, creation is under the curse, given to dust and ash. Nature reminds us of the world that was, but that's just it: that world is no more. Even the leftovers are infected. It is not enough to embrace the world that is, nor to remember that which was. My need, the great need of us all, is to know there is a better world to come.

Part 3

Breathless Expectation

Imagining the World That Will Be

One

Two days before the massacre, on April 14, I drove six hours from Blacksburg to Charleston, South Carolina, to baptize my friend Matt Christensen. It was a weekend spent on eternal things.

The sun was already hanging low to the west when I arrived, and we headed for the historic district to look around before nightfall. I hadn't toured Charleston in years, not since I was a child, but everything was familiar. The pastel-colored row homes that sat along the Battery, the USS *Yorktown* at rest in a distant port, and the expensive shops and restaurants lining the narrow streets — it was all as I remembered.

The glow of gradual sunset covered the district in warm hues. The streets ran with color and the buildings basked in the early evening light. Matt and I went about looking for the old church cemeteries where tour guides tell ghost stories. Our search led us down Philadelphia Alley, a narrow way between Queen Street and Cumberland. The air was pleasant and the breeze just right, neither cool nor warm. Flowers bloomed to the right and left of a brick and cobblestone path, and trees overhead shaded the walkway with early spring leaves.

It was a perfect, *perfect* moment. I felt as if I were floating through the alley, as if carried on the breeze. Every anxious thought and care dissolved. The busyness of my life in Blacksburg faded; I could not even remember what work awaited me when I returned. For an instant, there was no yesterday, no tomorrow. There was only now, glorious now, stretching out forever in front of me. This was heaven on earth, eternity breaking into time, a glimpse of the kingdom to come. I closed my eyes, breathed deeply, and tried to take it in, wonderfully lost in the sensation. I remember wishing I could grab hold of the moment and take it with me, to remember it in dark times. *If only I could hold on to this moment!*

It was no use, of course. The moment passed as we exited the alley at the other end. All that remained was a peaceful afterglow that followed me the rest of the day. Sunset shifted from yellow to orange and then to rouge as we came to St. Philip's on Church Street. Weathered stones dotted the graveyard, dating back as far as the 1600s.

"In hopes of a joyful resurrection," read one marker, "here rests the body of Col. William Rhett." The colonel has been hoping a long time: he died almost three hundred years ago. *Imagine resting in the same spot all these years.* Did he know he'd have to wait this long for a new body? Did he know his grave would be a tourist stop? I couldn't help but think of myself in his place. Will someone stroll past my plot one day and marvel, "Wow, three hundred years"?

I don't want to hope that long.

Who was this William Rhett? I wasn't up on my Charleston history. I knew only what I gleaned from the marker.

> He was a kind Husband
> A tender Father
> A faithful Friend
> A charitable Neighbor
> Religious constant worshiper of God
> He died suddenly but not unprepared.

As twilight overtook the day and we headed home for dinner and sleep, I thought about the colonel's epitaph. A good way to face one's end, I decided (may we all be so blessed): suddenly but not unprepared.

—

The next day Matt and I, and a few of his friends, headed to the beach for Matt's baptism. This day was different. Clouds were rolling in, winds were high, and the forecast called for storms. The once tall and rolling dunes were laid flat as countless tiny grains launched on the wind and scattered down the shoreline. We winced and laughed from sand stinging the backs of our legs. The salty air around us, in our ears and whipping our hair, was a constant assault. It never let up. A front was passing through, dragging colder days behind it. The chill had already settled over Blacksburg, and I was glad to be many miles south of there, if only for a few hours more.

We all faced the same direction, looking out over the sea, to keep the grit out of our eyes. I attempted a few words on baptism, but the howl of the wind was so strong, hardly anyone could hear. I gave up, and we waded out into the surf that was warm for mid-April.

It's ironic that an event so long on meaning is over in an instant, but a baptism is always only an instant. You cannot make it linger. You cannot hold people underwater. They go down and come up and that's it. Death and then life. Done. And as Matt went down into the water, I thought, *I bet Colonel Rhett wishes reality were as swift.*

After the baptism, we fought the cold front back to our cars, my friend Matt shivering as the wind blew him dry. I needed to get on the road. The work I forgot down Philadelphia Alley was now very much on my mind. I was firmly back in time now, eternity lost to the urgency of the moment. I had much to do back home, and still six hours to drive before I could start. After hugs and good-byes, I was on my way.

The temperature seemed to drop with every mile north as I struggled against wind gusts to keep my car in the lane. Along the Virginia border, the air was biting and the mountains dusted white. Snow pellets appeared in the beams of my headlights and beat against the windshield. *Was I really in the ocean today?*

I refused to give in to winter's last angry gasp. Straining, I reached beneath the passenger seat and pulled out a CD left over from the holidays. If nature wanted a Christmas party, I'd give her one.

> *... I brought some corn for popping.*
> *Lights are turned way down low.*
> *Let it snow, let it snow, let it snow.*[1]

I sang and laughed at the absurdity of Christmas in April as my car hurried down the interstate.

But songs and smiles would not be enough to stop what was going to happen. Spring would be cut short this year. The earth would harden overnight. Flowers that had been beautiful and young that day would be dead in the morning. *Do they know what is going to happen to them?*

Tomorrow would be bitter indeed.

It doesn't seem fair.

Two

I have often thought what a good and gracious thing it was for God to give me Philadelphia Alley, knowing as he did what was only two days away. God knew I would need some sign in the darkness that the world as it is, is not as it always will be. Indeed, many times during the week of April 16, my only happy thought was the memory of Charleston. Each time I drifted back in my mind, it was as though God were whispering in my ear, "Do not surrender to your sorrow, Matt. Remember Philadelphia Alley. This is a foretaste of the world that will be."

I am longing even now for another walk down that alley, another moment of heaven overlapping the earth. But I know I cannot have it. Not now, not yet. Even if I got in my car this instant and drove the six hours there, I would find nothing more than a narrow walkway, like any other walkway in the world, nothing special about it. The portal into heaven, flung open that day, has surely closed by now.

But not forever. For this is the future promised us in Scripture, heaven and earth merging into one, and I have glimpsed that happy world.

The apostle John, describing as best he could the ineffable Revelation, wrote:

> The seventh angel sounded his trumpet, and there were loud voices in heaven, which said: "The kingdom of the world has become the kingdom of our Lord and of his Messiah, and he will reign for ever and ever."[2]

Isn't this the longing that I feel, standing over Matt La Porte's grave, kneeling next to Baker's tomb? I groan with creation for the day they will rise, for the day Christ appears, when evil will flee and heaven and earth will be one. Jesus taught us to pray for this. "Your kingdom come," he said, "your will be done, on earth as it is in heaven."[3]

Our songs remind us,

> This is my Father's world: the battle is not done:
> Jesus who died shall be satisfied
> And earth and heav'n be one.[4]

The Bryants say they are stretched between two kingdoms, with children here and children there. The good news for Mark and Joyce is that one day they will not have to choose between kingdoms any longer. They will be pulled between the two no more. The kingdom of this world will become the kingdom of our Lord and of his Christ, and he will reign for ever and ever. And this will bring an end to the heavy, sinking sadness of this world.

The Bible implores us to dream about that day. Paul writes, "Let heaven fill your thoughts."[5] He says, "Our citizenship is in heaven. And we eagerly await a Savior from there, the Lord Jesus Christ."[6]

The apostle Peter, in one of Scripture's boldest enticements, says, "Set your hope fully on the grace to be given you when Jesus Christ is revealed."[7]

Fully, not in part. Set *all* your hope on this future grace, this one event.

And until we see this day, we long and we groan. Five times, in one way or another, Paul says we greatly anticipate this grace. He says, "We *wait eagerly* for our adoption"[8]; "[we] *eagerly wait* for our Lord Jesus Christ to be revealed"[9]; "by faith we *eagerly await* through the Spirit the righteousness for which we hope"[10]; "we *eagerly await* a Savior from [heaven]."[11]

And Paul says there is a crown awaiting him and "all who have *longed* for [Christ's] appearing."[12]

Longing is our life. And this is not a passive waiting. This is not a throwing up of the hands or a riding out of the world until Jesus returns. Paul and Peter and the other apostles did not toss earth out their back door like so much trash. Just the opposite. They embraced the world in all its pain and got busy pointing people to the bright future ahead. Earth had hope, a final ultimate grace in the coming of the King who would set things right.

Exactly what this day will look like, we do not know. We are given only glimpses. But they are grand glimpses indeed. John writes euphorically:

Then I saw "a new heaven and a new earth," for the first heaven and the first earth had passed away, and there was no longer any sea. I saw the Holy City, the new Jerusalem, coming down out of heaven from God, prepared as a bride beautifully dressed for her husband. And I heard a loud voice from the throne saying, "Look! God's dwelling place is among the people, and he will dwell with

them. They will be his people, and God himself will be with them
and be their God. 'He will wipe every tear from their eyes. There
will be no more death' or mourning or crying or pain, for the old
order of things has passed away."

He who was seated on the throne said, "I am making everything new!" Then he said, "Write this down, for these words are
trustworthy and true."[13]

That's about all the description we have, but it is more than
enough to make us long for the world that will be. And it is what
I need most in my grief: not answers, which hardly satisfy, but a
glimpse to make me groan, and an assurance that this groaning is
not forever. There is a better, certain kingdom to come.

Author Oswald Chambers says life for the follower of Christ
should be one of "breathless expectation."[14] We are always eagerly
looking ahead, forever tasting in advance the future grace and goodness of our God.

Some theologians believe that when Jesus returns he will restore the present earth to its original flawless design, casting out evil and whatever causes pain. Others suggest the creation is marred beyond repair, that God will wipe it away and start fresh with a new heaven and a new earth. The first theory resonates with Paul's teaching in Scripture; the second feels more consistent with Peter's writings.[15]

I have no idea who's right, nor do I see how it matters. If God means to fix the world, then our goal as his followers is to work toward that end, feeding the poor, eradicating disease, opposing injustice, rooting out evil. If God means to replace the world, the goal is the same. Whether we are helping create the world that will be, or merely painting a picture of it, our calling is the same. And it is clear. We must use our imaginations to see, and to help others see, the good future ahead.

Scripture says that "no eye has seen, no ear has heard, no mind has conceived"[16] what God has in store for those who love him. I once took this to mean I shouldn't bother trying to imagine it. What's the point? I thought. It's beyond knowing. I now think, Why *not* try? I'll come closer to conceiving what God has planned than if I make no attempt at all.

Children don't struggle with imagination as we adults do. Children dwell in it all day. Their world consists of it. Perhaps it is for this reason that Jesus said, "Truly I tell you, unless you change and become like little children, you will never enter the kingdom of heaven"[17] — you will never even imagine it.

The young also have no problem believing the impossible things their imaginations invent. Again, no wonder Jesus said, "Let the little children come to me, and do not hinder them, for the kingdom of heaven belongs to such as these."[18] For it was Jesus who taught that "what is impossible with human beings is possible with God."[19] And "all things are possible with God."[20] *All* things. If I can imagine it, and if it is good, then it is possible.

Do I believe this? Or do I breeze past the promise of a world without tears because it seems too good to be true? How much time do I spend anticipating the day when the dead will rise? Does resurrection appear to me as the certainty that it is? Or does it seem like little more than a weightless fairy tale wish?

Pain can make us cynics. It can rob us of faith in any future hope. We have to fight this. If a better world seems impossible, beyond that in which we can practically believe, then perhaps we need to humble ourselves, forget what we've learned, and become again like little children: rediscover imagination.

As a little boy, I fell in love with a British science fiction show called *Doctor Who* about an eternally optimistic time traveler from another world who hopped around the galaxies saving the universe from harm. Never did I think, "Well, this is absurd. Time travel has been proven impossible. Many scientists think life on other planets is statistically unlikely. Why waste time dreaming about such nonsense?" No, for me these wonders were more than possible. They were probable. And every week, I eagerly awaited the next adventure.

Doctor Who was canceled by the BBC in 1989 after thirty years on the air inspiring children like me. Soon after, at age fifteen, I became a Christian and entered a grown-up church world that was more concerned with answers than with possibilities. I learned what mattered was that I know how to reason with a skeptic, debate with an unbeliever, and explain any number of doctrines — some essential, most not. I heard many sermons on the depravity of the world that is, but few that foresaw the good world that will be. Instead of an imaginative faith, I received a dreary religion.

It took discovering Madeleine L'Engle's writings in my early twenties to remind me that imagination is good; it is God-given. (Even the titles of her books — *A Wrinkle in Time, A Wind in the Door* suggest that the seemingly absurd is wonderfully possible.) Of course, as with everything else God made, the imagination can be twisted and distorted into evil. But it is not intrinsically so. Romans 1:21 in the King James (the version I read as a new believer) says that human beings turned corrupt when they "became vain in their imaginations, and their foolish heart was darkened." I mistook this, and any number of other verses, to mean imagination was a thing I should fear. It is only so if used to create ideas counter to the kingdom that is coming. Otherwise, it is one of our greatest tools in tasting and seeing God's goodness in advance.

When the BBC revamped *Doctor Who* and brought it back in 2005, I was ready with a restored, childlike imagination. The show inspires me still. In a recent episode, one character said to the mysterious, time-traveling doctor, "I have seen the world inside your head and know that all things are possible." This should be our message on the earth. "We have glimpsed the future inside God's mind. We have not fully seen it, and our minds haven't fully conceived it. (No mind can.) But we've seen enough to know that he and his plan are very, very good. Together, let's imagine and work toward the world that will be."

Four

Much of our imagining of the new heaven and new earth will happen in community, in our small groups and worship gatherings. Some of us have more active imaginations than do others, and so we need each other to "see" the glorious future God has planned. We are tempted in pain to believe this world of sadness is all there is, or all there ever will be. At those times, we must lean on the creative faith of friends to show us brighter days ahead.

The evening after the massacre at Tech, I spent time with one of my church's student small groups. They gathered to worship, to pray for healing, and to remember Lauren McCain, a student and member of their group who was killed by Seung-Hui Cho. I went that night expecting to lend pastoral comfort to these mourning students. Instead, I sat at the back of the room and marveled at what I saw.

The worship was raw and real. Tears flowed freely. No one hid their pain or cared who saw it. I noticed a number of parents in the room, but none of us "older folk" were needed. We sat on the edges and watched these students lead themselves, remind each other that God was still good despite what had happened. Those closest to Lauren, and therefore the most shaken, were held and loved and comforted by the rest.

When song and prayer ended, no one went home. Someone broke out snacks, and pockets of conversation spread through the room. One brave soul chanced a joke, which freed the group to laugh, to know it was okay to smile in spite of pain. And so it went. So *they* went, moving naturally, casually, without any awkwardness at all, through the varied waves of emotion that come with grief. At times they laughed and played board games. At others they held one another and cried.

Through the night they went, and into the following day. In fact, they barely left each other's side for an entire week. They were together during the day, then fell asleep on the floor or on the couch at night. In the morning, they cooked breakfast and did it all over again. And I kept returning to them every free moment I got, simply to watch and to be near their warm spirits.

These students were more than a group; they were a family. And when a family faces loss, everyone comes together. Relatives stay by one another's side. Here was the family of God, brothers and sisters drawing in, drawing close, protecting and comforting their own. What a living illustration these students gave me of the kingdom that will be. "Blessed are those who mourn," Jesus said, "for they will be comforted."[21] "Blessed are you who weep now, for you will laugh."[22] I felt as though these were the early moments of heaven, as though I were watching God wiping tears from his children's eyes.

And these students—they came from so many different backgrounds and beliefs. Some were raised Baptist, others Pentecostal. There were Methodists and Presbyterians and Catholics alike. Some came from no church background at all. And yet they were all one, just as Jesus had prayed they would be.[23]

Isn't this the church at its best? Don't all our hearts ache for such a place to call home, a Spirit-bound, love-drenched community to which we completely belong? This is the image of the world that will be. Graham Tomlin, in a masterful little book called *The Provocative Church*, says:

> Christians are not meant just to try to do good, be nice and help the world work a little bit better. They are instead to act as sign-posts to another order, another way of life, another kingdom, which can be glimpsed in this world, but has not yet arrived completely.... Those who believe in God's kingdom and king-ship will want to act as signs of that kingdom, offering reminders, aromas, tastes of what it might mean to live under God's rule, not the iron law of sin and death.[24]

I smelled the aromas of heaven in that group. I tasted the goodness of God's rule. And I kept coming back for more. So will the world, I think, when our churches are ablaze with this holy imagination; when people walk through the door and hear us say, "Come in, come in! And let heaven fill your thoughts."

Five

I feel the aching every day, the groaning for the kingdom to come. How should I live in the meantime, until that longing is satisfied? Every generation has prayed theirs would be the one to usher in the world that will be. Yet all have died in unfulfilled hope. Perhaps ours will be the eyes that see Christ before we see death, but we cannot assume so much. Maybe tomorrow our sorrows will end, but maybe not. And so we must find a way to live well in a world that isn't.

Madeleine L'Engle, recognizing the need for such an approach to life, writes:

> We can surely no longer pretend that our children are growing up into a peaceful, secure, and civilized world. We've come to the point where it's irresponsible to try to protect them from the irrational world they will have to live in when they grow up.... Our responsibility to them is not to pretend that if we don't look, evil will go away, but to give them weapons against it.

> One of the greatest weapons of all is laughter, a gift for fun, a
> sense of play which is sadly missing from the grownup world.[25]

Laughter has returned to the Drill Field. The fall semester begins in a few days, and students who have come back early take to the grassy lawn for a lighthearted game of ultimate Frisbee. I pause to watch, to wonder at the sight, and to relish the welcome return of joy to this place of tears. Four months ago, laughter and fun would have been entirely inappropriate here. Now they make all the sense in the world. It is not as though these students have forgotten the memorial that rests only yards from where they play. They are surely very much aware of Norris in the distance. They are cognizant of death. Yet they run and leap and dive for a simple disc, caught up in the thrill of life.

From these students I learn that we need not enjoy life less for our groaning. Indeed, to groan is to play. And to play is to remind ourselves of the good and happy nature of the world that will be. In that coming kingdom, laughter and fun will always be appropriate. Joy will be the order of the day.

The world as it is now is troubled, yes, and thus we groan. But we do not have to hunker down, hole up in our sanctuaries, and hide from evil. We can, instead, dance and laugh and play, and let our enjoyment of life in the present be elevated by our anticipation of better things to come.

We are free to exult in the world that is without demanding more from it than it can offer. I can receive the good that comes my way without expecting *only* good. Life, for now, is a mix of wholeness and brokenness, and my experience of it will reflect that. I know I cannot have joy without suffering so long as this world endures. But that is the point, the meaning hidden in our play: this life will *not* endure; a better world is coming.

Six

August always feels like forgiveness to me. On a college campus, it is a time of beginning again at the start of a new school year. This year, however, we are still dealing with the old.

Today, Tech dedicates a permanent memorial to the victims of April 16. The old stones have been removed and offered as mementos to the families. In their places, new, larger chunks of limestone have been set in the familiar semicircle out in front of Burruss. On each slab is etched the name of a Hokie who is gone.

The ceremony starts at noon on a Sunday. We end our morning service early, as do churches all over the area, so members can attend the dedication. The sky, but for a thin haze, is clear. The sun is high and hot, unmerciful. This is typical late-August fare in Blacksburg.

I forgot sunscreen, and the ceremony is long. Several students faint from the midday heat and are helped off the field by friends. The thousands of us gathered on the Drill Field hear speeches reminding us to honor the goodness of the thirty-two we lost. I hope we will do that. But I also hope we will remember our dead in all their complexity. They were, as we all are, people both beautiful and flawed.

The friends and mentors killed here were not special because they were better. They were special because they were normal. They were ordinary, imperfect people who had good traits and bad, and we loved them as they were. Speaking of them in grandiose terms would only muddy our memory of them, and I want to remember them rightly.

I can recall, after my friend Baker died, feeling a strong need to think and speak of the man as he truly was, taking into account his virtues, yes, but also his vices. Though tempted otherwise by emotion, and by a deep desire to honor my friend, I insisted on total truth in remembering Baker. He would not have wanted people exalting him, and a glorified view of the man would have been untrue anyway. Baker, though deeply good, had his problems like any of the rest of us. Given that the theme of his life was how much we need God's grace, he would not have wanted us forgetting that this message applied to him as well.

At the funeral service for Baker, the pastor rightly said, "Baker really lived! Sometimes we were afraid he was living *too much*." The hundreds gathered at the church chuckled. They knew it was true. Baker had a mischievous thirst for adventure that sometimes got him in trouble. I was riding in the car with him once when he decided to ignore a Road Closed sign just to see what we would find. What we found were flashing blue lights from a police car up ahead.

Baker had his faults, for sure. Once, while on a road trip, we stopped at a convenience store for a snack. The special was two doughnuts and a cup of coffee for some price I don't remember. It was supposed to be a deal. Baker, however, wanted only one doughnut and asked the clerk if he might have his one doughnut and coffee at the special rate. "No," the clerk said, "You'll have to get two doughnuts if you want the deal." This made no sense to Baker. Why should he pay more for one doughnut than for two? Why wouldn't the special be anything *up to* two doughnuts and coffee for said price?

Stubborn as he sometimes was, Baker argued with the woman, unwilling to budge. Finally, I said, "Baker, forget it, *I'll* eat the extra doughnut! Let's go." Baker relented, but he grumbled back to the car and onto the highway.

I want to remember this about him. It is part of what made Baker who he was. He had problems like anyone. Oh, but he was wonderfully good as well. Baker had dedicated his life to ministry and was training for overseas missions work when he learned he had leukemia. He loved people as much as, and maybe more than, anyone I've met. He prayed more than most of us too, it seems, and for more people. After his death, Baker's parents found scores of names he'd scribbled on cards as reminders to pray.

And he was a constant friend. If only I had a log of all the hours Baker spent just listening to me as I worked through problems in my life. I deplore the term "best friend" because I do not like ranking people, but Baker certainly fit the description. He always helped, never hurt, my life and faith.

Over lunch with his parents one day, a few years after Baker died, I said, "Some people knew him as a hero, or as a guy who was passionate about missions. He certainly was those things. But I'm glad I got to know him simply as a friend. I feel like I really *knew* him."

"And he knew you," his mother said.

Yes. We knew each other, and we were good for each other. He was the free and wild one, I the cautious and reserved. Together, we kept each other from extremes. He challenged me to live. I challenged him to live a bit less. (I'm afraid, given the pastor's comment at the funeral, Baker won the challenge more times than I.)

I expect to see Baker again someday, and I'd like to recognize him when I do. How can I if I allow my memory of him to be blurred by a sanitized idea of the man that is not the true picture? Baker was a soul in need of mercy, no less than the rest of us. And of such will be the kingdom to come: real people who desperately needed and found the love and forgiveness of God. It is *God's* goodness, not our own, that we need to taste and see.

September 6. Madeleine L'Engle has died. She has not passed away, or passed on, or passed out. She has died. And as with my brother Preston, and as with Matt La Porte, I miss Madeleine even though we never met.

Appropriate that I got the news when I did: this evening, sitting in a training seminar on responding to grief and trauma. The news headline hit me like a punch to the gut. It read, simply, "Madeleine L'Engle, Children's Writer, Is Dead." Looking now at Madeleine's picture on the back of one of her books, I am filled again with that awful sense of wrongness about the world. Death is wrong. It shouldn't be.

After his wife died of cancer, C. S. Lewis wrote:

It is hard to have patience with people who say "There is no death" or "Death doesn't matter." There is death. And whatever is matters. And whatever happens has consequences, and it and they are irrevocable and irreversible. You might as well say that birth doesn't matter. I look up at the night sky. Is anything more certain than that in all those vast times and spaces, if I were allowed to search them, I should nowhere find her face, her voice, her touch? She died. She is dead. Is the word so difficult to learn?[26]

Search as I may, I will not find Madeleine anywhere. And only one thing will revoke and reverse this cold, cruel truth.

Eight

It is surely a failure of imagination that we do not think and speak more of resurrection. We the saints of present-day Christianity focus on the death of Christ to the near-absolute exclusion of his rising. Oh, we'll drag out the fact of his new life around Easter, but otherwise it sits collecting dust on the shelf. How much of our daily focus is geared toward the simple, shocking reality of resurrection?

Madeleine L'Engle's death renews in me the need to know that the story doesn't end here. If death is Christ's final chapter, then it is ours as well; we're still under the curse, for "the wages of sin is death."[27] And we're still dust returning to dust if Christ was not raised. Paul understood this. He strongly challenged the people of Corinth who were entertaining the idea of a kind of faith in Christ without a resurrection: "If the dead are not raised, then Christ has not been raised either. And if Christ has not been raised, your faith is futile; you are still in your sins. Then those also who have fallen asleep in Christ are lost. If only for this life we have hope in Christ, we are to be pitied more than all others."[28]

Pitied because we've prattled on about a future world while watching that world go to the grave, never to return. "But Christ has indeed been raised from the dead," Paul wrote, "the firstfruits of those who have fallen asleep. For since death came through a man, the resurrection of the dead comes also through a human being. For as in Adam all die, so in Christ all will be made alive. But in this order: Christ, the firstfruits; then, when he comes, those who belong to him."[29]

For Paul, the resurrection was essential. It was the great reversal of all that had gone wrong on the earth. It was the undoing of the curse. If there is no resurrection, then death reigns forever, God's creation is permanently marred, and evil ultimately wins. Dust returns to dust.

This is not a side issue of our faith. This *is* the faith. Without the resurrection there is nothing in which to hope. Madeleine L'Engle, Matt La Porte, Colonel Rhett, Baker Falls, Preston Rogers, my dad one day, myself—all are gone forever if the dead don't rise, and the world to come will be as cursed as the world that is.

We must learn to think and speak as if resurrection were the grandest and most wonderful truth in the world. It is.

Nine

I wish sometimes that the apostle Paul had been more graphic. Intellectually he has made the case for our need of new bodies, glorified after death. But some of us require more than mere intellect. We need our imaginations stirred. We need to taste and see. What is it about death, which is so horrible, so completely distasteful, that it would make my soul cry out for resurrection?

Currently there are two primary methods for dealing with the dead. One is bent on preservation, the other on destruction. Both have a horrible end. If you choose embalming, the goal is first to forestall decay, then to make your chilled self appear as lifelike as possible through artistry and deceit. Bacteria is a primary culprit in decomposition, a process that begins at the moment of death. Thus, upon arriving at the funeral home, you are promptly filled with preserving chemicals that displace your once-essential lifeblood. Your features then are set: eyes closed forever, mouth sutured shut. A makeup artist dresses you, positions your limbs, and paints you up. And you're ready for the show.

Of course, you've only tidied up and slowed down the inevitable. Embalming is temporary relief from rotting, but rot you shall. How fast is anyone's guess. A matter of weeks to many years, depending on several factors — temperature, humidity, and access to oxygen chief among them.[30]

One particularly foul stage in decomposition is putrefaction, the progression of which is horrific. Gases build in the body from bacteria at work. Skin blisters, tissues liquefy, and organs swell. Your face is no longer a face; you don't look like yourself.[31] Eventually your innards burst. Annie Dillard writes, "If you walk a graveyard in the heat of summer, I have read, you can sometimes hear — right through coffins — bloated bellies pop."[32]

Should you choose cremation, the process is this: A furnace is heated to a thousand degrees, give or take a few hundred, and you are sealed inside for a couple hours. Most believe the story ends there. But all the flames accomplish is the immolation of the flesh; swept from the oven, you remain as bits of bone. The crematory operator picks through the pieces, removing any large, inorganic lumps, any joint replacements or metal plates you received in your life. Put through a pulverizer, you then are ground to a fine powder, your final state.[33] This we call ash (an obvious misnomer), and at this the curse is fulfilled. So whether you choose embalming or cremation, you are dust returned to dust.

We in America, particularly the young, tend to label people morbid who think about these things. But I am merely commenting on the eventual experience of us all. Why should that be odd? And maybe we are meant to give attention to this. What if there is a message from God to us, hidden in the gory details of our end? What if, in what would be the ultimate irony, the curse itself is a signpost pointing to the cure—a cure we miss because we are always running from death, avoiding its very mention, or else speaking of it in sentimental terms?

Perhaps it is in honest reflection on death, a willingness to taste and see the results of the curse, that we find what we truly need: a deep, unutterable longing for the world that will be. Wherever we are laid, the oven or the earth, time will outlast our frame. We'll need new bodies in the kingdom to come. Resurrection, then, will be the unspeakably glorious vindication of having set all our hope on the day of Jesus Christ.

Ten

Nature has groaned again, sending a cyclone crashing into Bangladesh. Thousands are surely dead, tens of thousands without the basics of shelter and food and clean water. I am weeping with the prophet, "How long, LORD, must I call for help, but you do not listen?"[34] How much longer must this continue? When will you say, "Those are enough waves wrecking Bangladesh"?

What is the point of all this? Once again, I know all the clichés, the pat answers, that "the next big event on God's calendar is the return of Christ," that "the wait only seems long because we're human," and that "to the Lord a thousand years is only a day." But I'm not God and can't experience time as he does. For me, a day is a day, and a thousand years, a thousand. Peter says the Lord is merely showing us patience, hoping we'll repent.[35] What comfort is that to Bangladesh tonight?

Philip Yancey, when speaking to our church in April, said, "Trust a God who can redeem what now seems unredeemable. . . .

We remember [the day Jesus died] not as Dark Friday, Tragic Friday, or Disaster Friday—but rather as *Good* Friday. That awful day led to the salvation of the world and to Easter, an echo in advance of God's bright promise to make all things new."[36]

I am trying to trust, and in my heart I do. Yet in my mind tonight I see thousands of floating bodies, facedown in the sea or wrapped around trees stripped bare by wind and wave. I see a terrified child, separated from her mom and dad, screaming amid the rubble of the shack that was her home. And I struggle to imagine how this could be redeemed or made new, or could ever end in salvation.

From news reports, I hear that relief organizations such as World Vision are already gathering aid for Bangladesh. They are catching, and soon will be carrying, the echo in advance of the good new world that will be. They are encouraging the Bangladeshi—and they are encouraging me—to trust that even this can be redeemed.

Still, as I watch the news, I confess it is hard to live as I have said, to think of laughter, play, or fun. A game of Frisbee seems frivolous, self-indulgent, and absurd. All my talk of possibilities sounds to me like poetry: it is fanciful; it flows—but is it true?

There is no denying that things at present are bad. The curse has the run of the earth. One out of one dies, and often, like tonight, they go by the thousands, suddenly, horrifically. Evil and sadness permeate all that might otherwise be good. A quick online search turns up a host of tragedies:

- In Tanzania, there are two doctors for every 100,000 people.
- In Swaziland, the life expectancy is 32.6 years.
- HIV/AIDS orphans more than 6,000 children every day.
- Twenty-one children die of malnutrition and preventable diseases every minute.

- More than 840 million people in the world are malnourished.
- Six million children under the age of five die every year as a result of hunger.
- A third of the world has no exposure to God's Word.

Whatever hope we give in the face of such facts must be as earthly as it is heavenly. Merely quoting Scripture will not do. People need food and medicine and shelter if they are to catch any echoes in advance. Ours is only real hope if it speaks to the body as well as to the soul.

I am grateful for friends I've made through the years here at Virginia Tech, who are now spread around the world, offering this hope. I think of Lindsay in Mozambique. She teaches computer courses to employees of CARE International, a project serving orphans afflicted with HIV and AIDS. Lindsay says, "God has called me to serve others by helping meet their most basic needs. Even when the work feels futile, we can still do it in love, and God can still use it to further his purpose."

My friend Katie is in South Africa, living with a host family while helping educate a region devastated by AIDS. "There is so much hurt and pain in the world," she says, "how could someone *not* respond? Proverbs 31:8–9 says, 'Speak up for those who cannot speak for themselves, for the rights of all who are destitute. Speak up and judge fairly; defend the rights of the poor and needy.' I want to influence the world for good and empower others to act. I want to show love and grace to those in the direst need of it."

Kyle is in Mali, doing the holy work of building latrines. Better outhouses will stop sewage from seeping into the Malians' water supply. Could anything be more spiritual than giving people clean drinking water? "If anyone gives even a cup of cold water," Jesus said, "... that person will certainly be rewarded."[37]

All these friends have sacrificed greatly to give others hope. Kyle says, "Coming into this I was prepared for a lack of fellowship and physical support, but secretly I hoped it would turn out otherwise. It hasn't. It's just God and me here, but I think I'll end up stronger because of it. I feel now as if my four years at Tech were one big mountaintop experience. The mountain is great, but we aren't meant to stay there. The battle is in the valley, and that's where we're supposed to be. God reveals himself to us on the mountain; in the valley we share him with the world."

This is nothing less than the example of Jesus himself. "For you know the grace of our Lord Jesus Christ," Paul says, "that though he was rich, yet for your sake he became poor, so that you through his poverty might become rich."[38] This self-denying love that says, "Others before me," is the law of the kingdom to come. Acting in this way, my friends are giving the world a picture of the day of Jesus Christ. They are following the word of theologian N. T. Wright, who says, "Learn to think in terms of the world that is to be ... and of the people you will be within it, and then you will see clearly who you must be in the present time."[39]

I see it, but I cannot move to Mali or Mozambique, South Africa or Bangladesh. I have work here. I can, however, support those who are going. And I can look for other, simpler — yet no less meaningful — ways to serve.

For months I've considered supporting a child through Compassion International, World Vision, or some similar ministry. Busyness always distracts me though. And Lord knows there has been plenty of late to occupy the mind.

But tonight is at last the night. I reach for my laptop, pondering a comment my friend J. P. made to me once. He said, "Maybe we cannot *fix* the world—that's God's job—but we can *change* it." Maybe I cannot fix Bangladesh or any other disaster in the world. It's too big. It overwhelms. But I can help, I can bring change, even if only to one life.

I anticipated the joy of sponsoring a child; I did not expect I'd feel sadness too: in choosing one child, I am opting against thousands more. All their little faces stare at me, silently asking if I want them. I want them *all*. I'd feed and clothe and educate every one of them if I could.

The online process, designed for simplicity, takes me more than an hour. Clicking back and forth between pictures and profiles, I look for any sign that one child needs me more. Narrowing my options to three, I settle at last on Shukanto, eight years old, from Bangladesh. That he had waited the longest was the clincher for me. My thirty-two dollars a month will meet his basic needs, both physical and spiritual. Shukanto, whom I've already nicknamed "Shuki," will receive Bible teaching, nutritious food, medical care, health and hygiene education, recreational activities, tuition, and tutoring. In other words, his whole life will change for the better, and it cost me less than my cable bill.

This assumes, of course, that Shuki isn't among the thousands of Bangladeshi tonight for whom sponsorship is now a moot point. And all the happiness at helping this child is laced with the guilt of having left the others behind. All the right thinking I can muster—*I'm not God, I can't sponsor all those kids; others will have to help*—doesn't change how I feel. The fact remains: in choosing Shuki, I didn't choose Khokon, eleven years old and also of Bangladesh. I passed, as well, on eight-year-old Victorien, whom I left orphaned in Burkina

Faso, West Africa. Every hour, I check back to see if someone has taken the two I couldn't. So far, no one has.

Do Lindsay, Kyle, and Katie, in their respective African homes, go to bed at night thinking, "God, it's good to help these few. But, Lord, there are *so* many others"? Or do they rest easy, knowing they've done the bit they could and that it's now up to the rest of us to pitch in and paint a picture of the world that will be?

Time for sleep. I turn off the news and head upstairs. *What is Shuki doing this instant?* I wonder. The website said his favorite activity is running. *Is he running to tell his mom he has a sponsor?* I cannot know. I cannot go to him; I have work here. But I can send word ahead, like an echo in advance, that someone on the other side of the world cares. And as I learned this summer, the other side of the world is not so far away. Tonight it was only a few clicks away.

Eleven

It is Thanksgiving Day, and my parents are both sick with some virus, so the family isn't gathering—the first time in my thirty years that we haven't been together. At least we're all here still. That almost wasn't the case, as it is not for thirty-three families this Thanksgiving.

The Virginia Tech Corps of Cadets band, the Highty-Tighties, are in the Macy's Thanksgiving Day Parade, marching in a missing man formation for Matt La Porte. The crowds on either side of Thirty-Fourth Street stand to their feet and clap as the procession passes by, and I glance out the window of my living room toward the cemetery. Matt's birthday was two days ago. He would have turned twenty-one.

I would not have missed them for the world, but waiting on the Highty-Tighties to appear has made me late for dinner. I rush out the door and drive (faster than I should) to a church holding a community Thanksgiving meal. I am not going to eat but to fulfill a dream

I've had since childhood of serving dinner to the less fortunate. (I detest that label, but what other term would you use?)

From sponsoring Shuki I have learned that it is not only the receiver who experiences the goodness of God in a gift; it is also, and perhaps more so, the giver. And so I can think of no happier way to spend this day, since I cannot be with family, than preparing plates for the elderly, lonely, and poor.

Church members must have spent days preparing: I arrive to a spread of food fit for heaven itself. Mountains of turkey, stacked high on silver platters, pass from the kitchen to the serving table in the fellowship hall. Following the turkey are massive bowls of dressing and gravy, sweet and mashed potatoes, green beans and corn. On the dessert table, plates of pumpkin and sweet apple pie, garnished with dollops of whipped topping, await the hungry masses.

I find the organizer of this feast and ask how I can help. "As people come in," she says, "look for the older folks who need someone to get their plate for them." An elderly woman strolls in and takes a seat. I ask for her order, and she says roughly, "Gimme a lot of potatoes and gravy! I like a lot of potatoes."

"All right, ma'am. Extra potatoes for you."

"And I want pie made without any sugar," she says. "I can't have sugar."

Do they make such pies? I wonder. Indeed, I find a box of "no sugar added" apple pie among the desserts and cut the lady a slice.

"I want to get a plate of food to go when I leave. Can I do that?" she adds.

"I'll see to it."

Throughout the meal, I check up on the woman to see if she needs anything, and each time I do, she seems a bit more polite, a touch happier. When she stands to leave, she asks, "Are you a Hokie?"

"Why, yes, I am."

"I've never been a Hokie," she says, "but I'm going to pull for them now."

"We'd be grateful," I return, smiling. In an hour's time, I've watched this lady's countenance change completely, and all she needed was someone to fix her plate. She only needed extra potatoes. Just an hour's kindness from a stranger.

What could we accomplish in *two* hours? A day? A whole week of this? Or a lifetime? Ancient philosopher Philo of Alexandria said, "Be kind, for everyone you meet is facing a great battle." What burden was I privileged to make lighter for this woman today? What sadness was made less acute for her, if only for an hour? Did she taste the goodness of God in that apple pie with no sugar? Will she taste it again in the food she's taking home?

Paul says, "Always try to be kind to each other and to everyone else."[40] Goodness toward all — this is the way of the coming King: he is kind to all, even "to the ungrateful and wicked."[41] To spread kindness indiscriminately in his name is to spread the kingdom itself. It is to announce to the world, to friend and foe alike, "Great news! God is good, and the world to come is good. Come taste and see in advance."

———

Among the last to leave the church is an elderly woman, perhaps in her eighties. She pauses to say thanks on her way out the door. "This community dinner is such a blessing to me," she says. "It gives me people to be with on the holiday. I don't have anyone anymore. My husband died nine years ago, and the last member of my family, my brother, passed away this year. So it's just me now. *Thank you* for serving this meal!"

Despite the obvious, understandable sadness I see in her eyes, the woman's face is bright with joy. She smiles graciously and seems so alive here at the close of her life. What compounded grief this woman has known: her parents are gone, her siblings too; her mate; and doubtless many friends. She doesn't mention her children. Are they gone as well, or far away? She is alone, and yet she smiles. What saves this woman from despair?

I want to ask, though I cannot find a way. *Everyone you love is dead, and soon you will die as well. How are you happy despite being sad?* I could ask the apostle Paul the same. His troubles were so varied, constant, and extreme that they sound fictitious, completely over the top. He says:

Five times I received from the Jews the forty lashes minus one. Three times I was beaten with rods, once I was pelted with stones, three times I was shipwrecked, I spent a night and a day in the open sea, I have been constantly on the move. I have been in danger from rivers, in danger from bandits, in danger from my own people, in danger from Gentiles; in danger in the city, in danger in the country, in danger at sea; and in danger from false believers. I have labored and toiled and have often gone without sleep; I have known hunger and thirst and have often gone without food; I have been cold and naked. Besides everything else, I face daily the pressure of my concern for all the churches.[42]

The hardship took its toll. Paul said at one point, "We were under great pressure, far beyond our ability to endure, so that we despaired of life itself."[43] Existence for Paul was at times a burden. Not even worth it, it seems. He would have preferred death. And yet this same man said, "Rejoice in the Lord always. I will say it again: Rejoice!"[44]

He described himself as "sorrowful, yet always rejoicing."[45] How did he manage such a tricky balance?

How can I?

I want to ask this woman before me, but I can't find the words, and soon she is out the door, on her way home to be alone. On my way to do the same, I think through what Paul had to say about heaven: "To be away from the body," he wrote, is to be "at home with the Lord."[46] Is this what kept him going through his pain, the thought of his soul's soon-coming reunion with Christ? "I desire to depart and be with Christ," Paul said, "which is better by far."[47] Not just better; better *by far.*

Perhaps this disembodied state is not the goal; resurrection to immortal flesh and to a new heaven and a new earth, with God's glory for its light — this is the goal. But could it be that even the curse is laced with hope? Might even death have a bright side?

And is this the cause of the light in that old woman's face today? Her friends and family are gone, but soon she will be alone no more. Though she will sleep, she will be kept. She will shed her tired body, but she will be present with the Lord. And this is better. Better by far.

Twelve

Tonight, while decorating the Christmas tree, I was struck by the ridiculous nature of the whole thing. Move a dying tree, decapitated at the roots, indoors; wrap little lights around it; hang shiny things from it; and feel all warm and fuzzy while doing so. This must rank among the more bizarre rituals we humans have. I smiled at the thought but went on placing a miniature Hokie football helmet on a branch.

Probably any celebrating would look odd to some after this year. Certainly this was true after September 11, 2001. Everyone was asking, "What is appropriate? Do we go on with this event or that?" There was talk of canceling the Oscars that year; instead, the producers opted for a toned-down awards show.

At the time, I was working for a radio station, and we were asking the same question. At the holidays, we thought, "Do we go on with our Christmas format?" Yes, we decided. Of all years, Christmas — celebration of any sort — was sorely needed.

I had the job of selecting all the songs, a process that lasted from early October to Thanksgiving. Every day, for nearly two months (and then a month more when the songs played on the air), I heard familiar Christmas tunes learned in childhood. And after the fifteenth version of "O Come, O Come, Emmanuel," I began to actually hear the words:

> O come, Thou Day-spring, come and cheer
> Our spirits by Thine advent here;
> Disperse the gloomy clouds of night,
> And death's dark shadows put to flight.

How could I have hummed this tune all my life without ever consciously observing the lyrics?

> O come, Desire of nations, bind
> In one the hearts of all mankind;
> Bid Thou our sad divisions cease,
> And be Thyself our King of Peace.

This is a picture of the world to come, and at Christmas everyone is singing about it! How many, like me, go on year after year without realizing what they are singing?

Christmas that year for me lasted three months — ninety days spent exulting in the world that will be. I learned through that experience that we must celebrate, even when it seems to make little sense. *Especially* when it seems to make little sense.

Today I saw on Facebook that Derek O'Dell has indeed decked the halls. The balcony of his apartment is draped in Christmas lights that say "VT" and that take the form of the familiar ribbon people wore in support of Tech after April 16. A lighted snowman waves from the deck and wishes folks a happy holiday. Celebrating after a year of pain: this makes so much sense to me.

When we celebrate, we remind ourselves and those around us that this world of sadness is not all there is, and not all there will be. The world to come will be a time of constant rejoicing. No more tears. No more death. No more pain. No April 16 or September 11. No Holocaust. No stones. No dust and ash. We help people imagine this future reality when we celebrate in breathless expectation of it.

In *Cold Tangerines*, author Shauna Niequist writes:

> I believe in a life of celebration. I believe that the world we wake up to every day is filled to the brim with deep, aching love, and also with hatred and sadness. And I know which one of those I want to win in the end. I want to celebrate in the face of despair, dance when all we see on the horizon is doom. I know that Death knocks at our doors and comes far too early for far too many of us, but when he comes for me, I want to be full-tilt, wide-open, caught in the very act of life. I think that's what we're here for, not for a passive, peaceful life, but to stand up in the face of all that lacks peace and demand more.[48]

And to know there *will* be more. It is the certain future to come. We must celebrate it, no matter how odd this celebrating may look.

Thirteen

We don't need to wait for a holiday in order to celebrate. Any day will do.

When I was twelve, I auditioned for a role in Thornton Wilder's *Our Town* at our community theater. Can't remember where I got the idea or, being a shy child, the courage, to do it. The directors gave me the part of Joe Crowell, the newspaper boy for the fictional Grover's Corners, New Hampshire. All told, I had about ten lines of dialogue, so most of my time at rehearsals was spent watching others' characters come to life. *Our Town* is the simplest of stories about the most ordinary of lives performed with the sparsest of sets. In fact, there *isn't* any set. Just a blank stage and a few props. The point of it all, I think, is to show the wonder of the everyday, the grandeur in little things all around us that often go unnoticed.

In act 3, Emily Webb, who has died, is given the chance to relive one day of her life. She chooses her twelfth birthday, which was rather poignant for me, since I also was twelve at the time. Not only does Emily live the day over; she watches herself doing so and realizes with shock and sadness how much she missed at the time—how much we all miss in our daily rush through routine. "I can't look at everything hard enough,"[49] she says, trying to absorb the glory she overlooked in life. Her mother rushes about, preparing breakfast, barely noticing Emily at all. "Oh, Mama, just look at me one minute as though you really saw me. Mama! Fourteen years have gone by!—I'm dead!—You're a grandmother, Mama—I married George Gibbs, Mama!—Wally's dead too. Mama! His appendix burst on a camping trip to Crawford Notch. We felt just terrible about it, don't you remember?—But just for a moment now we're all together—Mama, just for a moment let's be happy—Let's look at one another!"[50]

Almost twenty years have passed since our little production of *Our Town*, but to this day, when I read the script (and I still have mine), I can hear the voice and inflection of the actress who played Emily. I can still hear her distress. It moved me profoundly as a child, and it moves me even now.

Emily says, sobbing, "It goes so fast. We don't have time to look at one another. I didn't *realize*. So *all* that was going on and we never noticed!"[51] She half turns to the Stage Manager, who also is a main character in the play and who also is watching this day lived over. She says to him, "Take me back—up the hill—to my grave. But first: Wait! One more look! Goodbye. Goodbye, world! Goodbye, Grover's Corners—Mama and Papa—Goodbye to clocks ticking—and my butternut tree! and Mama's sunflowers—and food and coffee—and new-ironed dresses and hot baths—and sleeping and waking up!"[52] Throwing her arms open as if to hug the world, Emily exclaims, "Oh earth, you're too wonderful for anyone to realize you!"[53] Then more quietly she asks the Stage Manager, "Do any human beings ever real-ize life while they live it — every, every minute?"

"No," the Stage Manager says. "Saints and poets maybe — they do some."[54]

I doubt the decision was conscious at the time, given that I was twelve, but watching that scene played out over and over, night after night in rehearsals, I determined to live this way. To be a saint and a poet, if only that I might see and celebrate the ordinary.

This is still my desire. I fail miserably in the attempt, but I do try. This spring has intensified my longing to live in the moment and not miss or take for granted one single instant. It's all so precious, worth rejoicing in. When I drink my coffee in the morning, I try not to do so in a hurry, rushed to make it out the door to some meeting. In the evenings, when the day is done, I attempt to savor and not merely read a good book before bed. Again, I probably fail more times than I succeed, but I'm trying, and hopefully I'm better for the effort.

Less than three weeks after the massacre at Tech, Derek O'Dell wrote on his Facebook page, "Over the past 18 days it has been hard for me not to think about what has happened. Before, when I would close my eyes, it would always be something meaningless that I would think of in my daydreams. Now when I close my eyes, I see my life, which has come to be more meaningful than ever. When you wake up each morning, don't be unhappy about the early alarm; be grate-ful that you have lived through another day. I know on the morning of April 16th I did not do this, but ever since, it's hard not to."

Before heading home in May at the end of the semester, he wrote, "Have a great and safe summer. Enjoy life, because every moment is beautiful and precious."

The apostle Paul says we are saints.[55] This being so, and if the

Stage Manager was onto something, then we of all people should be those who realize life while we live it — "every, every moment."

When someone asks, "Why do you get so excited about a sunset?" I can say, "Because it's lovely, and because love and beauty are echoes of the world that was, and echoes in advance of the world that will be."

What a picture of heaven we give the world just by taking joy in what others overlook. Paul says, "So whether you eat or drink or whatever you do, do it all for the glory of God."[56] Do it all as you would on that day when Christ returns. Do it all as if in celebration of the good King's return and of our loved ones raised. Even simple things like food and drink become inexpressibly glorious in this light. All is cause for celebration. In the world where we are headed, where pain and suffering are forgotten, *everything* is reason to rejoice.

Fourteen

I finish my thoughts on celebration and stop to check the day's head-lines on TV. "Breaking News: Terror in Omaha." Another massa-cre, this one at a shopping mall. Nine people dead, including the shooter.

Much of the reporting is eerily familiar. One survivor says the shots sounded like a nail gun, which he assumed at first was the noise of construction work in the mall. The mayor of Omaha, as if reading a transcript from Virginia Tech, says, "You never think something like this will happen in your town." News anchors use the same descriptors — "troubled," "depressed" — as were ascribed to Seung-Hui Cho, as if these are sufficient for explaining (or explain-ing away) evil.

All in all, though, the load of reporting is lighter this time. Is this the result of the lower death toll? Are we less bothered by the thought of nine dead, as opposed to thirty-three? The age of the victims, perhaps? We glorify youth, so does the idea of college students killed move us more than a story about some older people shot at a mall? Or is it simply that these events, while never less horrific, are becoming more common? The news is no longer new.

In any case, I cannot let myself be lulled into silent acceptance or hopeless resignation. Whether they're the rule or the exception, events like today, and April 16, and Columbine, and any tragedy in the world, have no place in the world that will be. Whether they be young or old, the dead were never meant to be so. They've succumbed to the curse, and I cannot grow numb to that fact, no matter how many similar stories I hear. And certainly a number should not matter. Thirty-three or one, any life lost is a tragedy. Even one is a massacre.

Last month, a Virginia Tech student fell from the seventh floor of his residence hall and died later at the hospital. Whether an accident or suicide, I do not know; investigators haven't ruled. I do know, however, that we moved on rather quickly from that loss — no ribbons or flowers or Hokie stones — and most of the major news outlets passed on the story altogether.

In my journalism classes, I learned that members of the media have a saying that crudely, yet somewhat accurately, portrays editorial decisions in newsrooms: "If it bleeds, it leads." Perhaps that should be amended to say, "If it bleeds *badly*, it leads." Doesn't rhyme, but it's more precise.

Clearly we believe in a sum of pain: a million starving children is a crisis worse than one starving child. Is it? C. S. Lewis is a help here. He writes:

> There is no such thing as a sum of suffering, for no one suffers it. When we have reached the maximum that a single person can suffer, we have, no doubt, reached something very horrible,

but we have reached all the suffering there ever can be in the universe. The addition of a million fellow-sufferers adds no more pain.[57]

Or as Proverbs says, "Each heart knows its own bitterness, and no one else can share its joy."[58] We each suffer our own pain, and that is all, and so our perception of a sum of pain is simply that: perception.

Philip Yancey, after passing through a tent of sympathies at Virginia Tech, wrote in an email:

Each of the 33 who died (yes, including the killer Cho) has a space inside the tent, and friends have left mementos such as a baseball, a teddy bear, a Starbucks cup. As I walked through the tent, I realized what the news media does to our perceptions. I had thought of a group of 33 people who died, "the worst mass killing in U.S. history," as television kept announcing. Walking past the individual memorials, I encountered one person, and another, and another, and another — 33 individuals, not a group.

One is as bad as thirty-three. And thirty-three is merely one, thirty-three times over.

Yet I remember my reaction on the morning of April 16, as news began to break. Reports of one dead in a dormitory didn't do much in me. If anything, I felt annoyed, frustrated at how this might mess with my schedule for the day. Eight dead bothered me a bit more, but it wasn't till the count reached twenty that the sadness hit and the darkness fell. I say this to my shame. Must it take so many to make me weep?

I should take my cues from Jesus. He exemplified concern for the individual. Yes, he fed the five thousand (and later the four thousand). Yes, he healed the ten lepers. But most of his miracles involved the one. A widow who has lost her only son. A blind man who begs for his sight. A woman who has bled for twelve years. These are the *ones* for whom Jesus felt compassion. Do we think he would have us live any differently today?

The merest hint of what makes God good is that he does not love as we do. His concern is for the one, not only the masses. If I have any hope of knowing and experiencing this goodness, I must learn to love as God does. In the kingdom to come — in *his* kingdom — even one matters. The world that will be should excite us, not because the throngs will have had their suffering healed, but because even one in pain was too many.

Fifteen

"Can't we just move on?" I've heard this question a lot this semester. It seems to come—though I can't be sure—from those least affected by the tragedy. There is a normal, natural fatigue with April 16. One grows weary of bearing a grief no longer felt. Once healing has occurred, there is a good and healthy desire to enjoy life once again. Some here are to that point.

But if by "move on" we mean "leave behind," this is something we can never do. The change to our campus is permanent. The thirty-two stones out in front of Burruss are proof of that. And those most closely associated with that terrible day do not wish to move on. They lost their friends and mentors; to move on is to forget. That'd be like me forgetting Baker, forgetting Preston. God forbid I ever do so. Imagine telling a witness to the massacre, or the families of the dead, "Can't we just move on?" It would be callous, to say the least.

But I understand the desire. Once I heard that a permanent memorial was going up in place of the makeshift stones, and in the same spot — at the focal point of campus where you cannot miss it — I grumbled. *Can't they put the thing someplace else, somewhere less obvious, less at the center of attention? Do we have to see this every time we come to the Drill Field?*

Where did I think they ought to put it? Where would you hide a memorial like that? *Why* would you hide it? In retrospect, I think the school made a wise decision: embrace the pain; own it. And I believe my desire that they do otherwise was hope against hope that we could wipe away the stain of spring, that enough time would pass so that we could get on with life as before. Then, perhaps, the tragedy would fade into surrealism, forgotten like a bad dream once we've awakened.

This is not an option. This sadness could have happened anywhere, on any campus. But it didn't. It happened here, and as Charles Steger, president of Virginia Tech, said, "We now own it forever."[59]

April isn't going away. We can never simply "move on" as if it didn't happen. But "move forward"? Yes, we must. How, though, and how quickly? How do we deal with April without being defined by it? Talk too much about the tragedy, and we risk retraumatizing people who've begun to heal. Talk too little, and we silently suggest everything's better now: "Life goes on!"

I think the burden is on us who have healed to help those who are still stuck in grief, putting aside the selfish desire to forget. Especially if we belong to Christ. His example is the essence of self-denial, ignoring personal wishes in order to aid those in need. And the apostle Paul says the church is a body. We are each an individual part of that body, but we are not separate from the other parts. Consequently, "if one part suffers," as he says, "every part suffers with it."[60] Rip a toenail from the skin underneath, and it is not only your toe that stings. Your whole body is attendant to the pain. In the church, if one member of the body hurts, all the members hurt with it.

So we move forward after April, yes, but only at a pace acceptable to the most injured among us. Love is the rule of the world that will be, and love waits for the wounded. Even one left behind is too many.

Sixteen

When tragedy happens, questions go from intellectual to emotional, from theoretical to personal. And often the questions are agonizing. As this year comes to an end, I am reflecting on the questions I've heard students asking here: "Where are my friends now? In heaven or hell? I don't think so-and-so believed in Jesus."

Asking is a part of learning. It is a means of coming to grips with the real world, and for that reason I never discourage the questions. Neither do I, however, answer them, not because I'm afraid to answer, but because I cannot. I did not know any of the victims personally, and even if I had, it is doubtful I would know what transpired between them and God in their final days on earth — and God would have known these were their last days. So I have no way of knowing who is where or where anyone should be. This is a question for God, and I am not him.

Furthermore, Jesus cautions us against becoming too consumed by such musings. First-century Israelites had, we think, a less developed theology of heaven and hell than we do today, so their first thought might not have been, "Is so-and-so in hell?" But they did, in times of tragedy, ask other related questions, such as "Were those folks killed because they were worse people than we are?" In Luke 13 Jesus answers:

> *"Do you think that these Galileans were worse sinners than all the other Galileans because they suffered this way? I tell you, no! But unless you repent, you too will all perish. Or those eighteen who died when the tower in Siloam fell on them — do you think they were more guilty than all the others living in Jerusalem? I tell you, no! But unless you repent, you too will all perish."[61]*

Jesus says the real question, the thought that should preoccupy us, is not "What of them?" but "What about me?" I imagine Jesus on the Drill Field, the day after the massacre, hit with the questions "What about these thirty-three, Jesus? Why them, and are they in heaven or hell?" And I picture Jesus responding, "This is not your concern. You should be thinking of your own condition. If this had been you — as it will be one day — are you prepared?"

What about me? The marker at Colonel Rhett's grave reads, "He died suddenly but not unprepared." Could this be said of me if today is my day? Am I following Jesus with my actions, not just my words, living as if I truly believe he is the coming King? And if I find that I am not living this way, am I willing to change?

Among the greatest comforts to me after Baker died was the certainty I had in the way Baker had answered these questions. Of all the people in my life, I was most sure of his faith, which he demonstrated daily. I knew where Baker was and did not need to fear for him in my grief. Are we leaving this peace to those who will follow us?

Jesus says unless we repent, we will surely perish. If resurrection is the door into the world that will be, then repentance is the key to that door. Without it, there is no way through. The door is locked.

We are much too put off by the term *repent*, perhaps for having heard preachers screaming it on TV. The word simply means to turn. That's it. To simply turn around, having found that we were going in the wrong direction. If we find we are living as if we were God, then we turn and worship him who is. If we discover we are living contrary to the manner God intended, then we turn and live as a citizen of heaven would. We forsake hatred, embrace forgiveness. We give without thought of receiving in return. We love God and the people he has made.

It was Jesus who modeled this, and it was Jesus who said, "I am the way and the truth and the life. No one comes to the Father except through me."[62] Each of us must answer the question: not "What about them?" but "What about me?" Have I embraced the King of the world that will be?

Seventeen

December 22, 2007. For us in the Northern Hemisphere, this is the winter solstice, the shortest day of the year in terms of sunlight. Sounds depressing, I suppose, except for what it signals: there is a limit to the darkness. Tomorrow there will be more light than today. And the next day, even more. Night is on a leash; it grows longer for a while but must eventually yield to the day.

This has been a year of extremes, times of brilliant joy but also of terrible sadness, and there were moments in the spring when I wondered if night would overtake the day and light would go out altogether. The psalmist felt this fear, the dread of darkness closing in, when you're suddenly no longer sure which side is going to win. "Look on me and answer, LORD my God. Give light to my eyes, or I will sleep in death."[63] This is more than poetry. I hear panic in David's voice, the surprising uncertainty that wonders if maybe there will be no happy ending this time.

I've echoed David's prayer many times since April, and still many times more over the fifteen years of my life with Christ. There have been days when the light has nearly gone out. But there is always the solstice. There is always a time when God says to the blackness, "That is enough. Night, you have grown long and proud. You must retreat."

I am grateful for this little clue creation gives, that darkness has a limit. It reminds me that evil also has a limit. God will only let the world grow so dim before he says, "Enough." He will only let *my life* grow so dim before he says, "Enough." He knows when it is time for solstice.

So there is reason to hope for next year, even as I reflect on the one that is passing away. Darkness may have advanced for a little while, but today is the winter solstice.

Eighteen

The family is having Christmas on the coast this year. The air is warm and nearly still along the shore. Rain is several hours away, but the first signs are already on the horizon. Far out over the Atlantic, clouds appear, thin and inconsistent like the back-and-forth strokes of a drying paintbrush. The muted sun is setting behind them. The day and the year are nearly done.

I walk along the sand, avoiding the chilly late-December tide pushing toward the dunes, listening to Christmas tunes through earphones.

> *Noel, Noel, Noel, Noel,*
> *Born is the King of Israel!*[64]

Somewhere I read that historians believe "Noel" is a shortened form of "Now all is well." That night when Jesus was born — when light shined on a people living in darkness — that night was "the first Noel," the first "Now all is well."

But all is *not* well, not yet. Not even close. This year has been a screaming reminder of that.

I spoke with Derek O'Dell last week — "Still doing well," he said, "a little better every week." I asked him about his Christmas lights. "I'm trying to celebrate," he said, "but it's hard whenever I think of the families of students and faculty here who lost someone."

And earlier today I received an email from Mark Bryant. He wrote, "Today, Christmas Day, we had breakfast together as a family with the reading of the Luke Christmas story. Then we exchanged gifts. Around noon, Joyce and I visited the graves, cried, and then went home for other family activities. We remember the past, enjoy the present, and prepare for the future."

And oh, how I wish that future were here now. The apostle John wrote, "The darkness is passing and the true light is already shining."[65] Perhaps. But night still has a ways to go, it would seem, and sunrise takes awhile.

Yes, the year is passing, but in countless little ways it will be with me all my life. I had a grilled cheese for lunch the other day and remembered Matt La Porte. Will it ever again be only a sandwich to me? I see a ladder leaned against a roof, and I think of Dad.

I read in the news just last week that a billionaire from Wisconsin fell through the roof of his home while checking the progress of construction on his garage. He died of massive head injuries, the story said. That could have been my dad and my story this Christmas.

What could ever make this okay? What could bring the Sarvers back to Sinking Creek, heal Bangladesh, or vindicate the hopes of the patient Colonel Rhett? What could comfort broken hearts back at Tech?

Surely not answers.

It was not answers that soothed Job's anguished soul. It was

God's presence. As author John Piper says, "God is the gospel."[66] Not intellectual solutions but God himself. God showed up, and Job experienced him as good. That's really what Job wanted, and what he needed.

Likewise, I doubt heaven will provide answers to all our questions. More likely we'll simply forget what questions we had. Caught up in wonder, we'll cover our mouths and say with Job, "I spoke of things I did not understand."[67] And there before our King, we'll bask in a goodness so real, so exquisitely experiential, that April 16, and September 11, and the Holocaust, and every other dark and evil day, will dissolve in the light. And for that day we wait in breathless expectation.

The Christmas account in Luke tells the story of Simeon, a man who had spent his life waiting, "waiting for the consolation of Israel."[68] The Scriptures say, "It had been revealed to him by the Holy Spirit that he would not die before he had seen the Lord's Messiah."[69] When at last Simeon held the infant Jesus in his arms, he worshiped joyfully:

> "*Sovereign Lord, as you have promised,*
>   *You may now dismiss your servant in peace.*
> *For my eyes have seen your salvation,*
>   *which you have prepared in the sight of all nations:*
> *a light for revelation to the Gentiles,*
>   *and the glory of your people Israel.*"[70]

Simeon wasn't looking for answers or for an immediate resolution to his pain. He only wished to glimpse that distant hope that might let him die in peace. He only needed to know the world would be all right someday, even if not today.

I sensed this hope two days ago when stopping by the cemetery on my way out of town. Matt La Porte has his permanent headstone now. Otherwise, little about the place has changed. The lump in the ground over Matt remains. A bit less pronounced, but there nonetheless. The grass continues its struggle too, despite recent rains. It is as though the earth is fighting back, refusing to cover and forget about Matt.

Matt's family and friends refuse as well. The grave shows signs of frequent visits. Flowers lay here and there, along with two small chunks of Hokie stone, a couple of candy canes, a Christmas wreath, and a red cardinal tree ornament. And of course the toy jet that's been there since spring. It sits as an icon at the head of the plot, announcing to the world that death is not the end of Matt's dreams. An interruption, yes, but not the end. Matt may yet fly that plane and share another grilled cheese with his friend Chris.[71]

I ache for that day and hold to its promise of consolation. I groan with creation, swell like the sea before me, in hopes of that time when all will be well. Until then, I live as the Bryants live, remembering the past, embracing today, and preparing for the world that will be.

I don't know why that world is so slow in coming, why so many sparrows must fall to the ground in the sight of God, and yet still he waits. What is gained by this delay?

The apostle Paul says, "I consider that our present sufferings are not worth comparing with the glory that will be revealed in us."[72] What lies ahead, he means, is worth the wait. I confess, some days this is difficult to believe. It is then that I lean on Paul's imagination, and then that I look to the creative faith of John. He comes to the end of the Revelation and finds the end so good, he can hardly wait. Jesus says, "Yes, I am coming soon," to which John replies, "Amen. Come, Lord Jesus."[73]

I would argue "soon" is a point of view. Yet it is the waiting that accentuates the longing, intensifies our groaning. It is the anticipation, growing greater by the day, that makes our hearts cry out with John's. This hope deferred is itself an experience of God's goodness, for if we did not expect that God was good, why should we look for him so long?

Until the cries for Christ to come are answered, we should be busy painting pictures of how that day will be. Annie Dillard writes, "After Michelangelo died, someone found in his studio a note to his apprentice, in the handwriting of his old age: 'Draw, Antonio, draw, Antonio, draw and do not waste time.'"[74]

This is a message to us. Whatever Jesus meant by "soon," it is surely sooner now than ever. Time is precious, and it is short. Let us paint now, and with all the imagination we can muster. And if we die before the picture is done, may we be found with brush in hand, eyes fixed ahead, looking toward the day when all the world will say, "Where, O death, is your sting?"

I value your thoughts about what you've just read.
Please share them with me. You'll find contact information
in the back of this book.

Acknowledgments

Many wonderful people contributed to the creation of this book. My deep thanks to all for their efforts.

To my agent, Greg Daniel, who has no idea how nervous I was to show him the initial drafts. His guidance and praise (and patience with my many emails) proved crucial to my sanity and faith. It is a pleasure working with him.

To the entire Zondervan team, for putting their hearts and minds into producing a book of the highest quality. Angela Scheff, my editor, was wise and considerate in her approach, and was the first to encourage me to write this book; Becky Shingledecker, my developmental editor, took great care in overseeing the finer points of the manuscript and was so gracious with my bouts of paranoia over details; Beth Shagene designed a beautiful interior that perfectly suits the tone and subject matter of the book; Curt Diepenhorst created a wonderful cover with many layers of meaning; and Karen Campbell created and coordinated the plan for PR. My thanks to them all. Their enthusiasm fueled mine.

To Derek O'Dell and the Bryants, for trusting me with their stories. My conversations with them are cherished memories and highlights of my time spent working on this book.

To Chris Backert and Brian McLaren, whose early optimism paved the way toward publication.

To Jason and Katie Snook who opened their home to me as a writer's retreat, a gift that came at just the right time. I'm tempted to write a sequel simply for another week of their hospitality.

To friends and family I neglected during long hours of writing. I thank them for their understanding and for cheering me on.

To the pastors, staff, and saints of New Life Christian Fellowship. I can't imagine serving with better people.

Notes

About the Book
1. Annie Dillard, *The Writing Life* (New York: HarperPerennial, 1990), 68.

Preface
1. Matthew 6:25–34.
2. Matthew 10:29 NLT.
3. Psalm 34:8.

Part 1
A Heavy, Sinking Sadness:
Embracing the World That Is
1. 1 Corinthians 15:55.
2. Ecclesiastes 3:11.
3. Genesis 3:19.
4. Philippians 1:21.
5. 1 Corinthians 15:26.
6. Elie Wiesel, *Night* (New York: Hill and Wang, 1958), 34.
7. Ibid., 33.
8. Ibid., 34.

9. *Holocaust* is formed by the mixing of two Greek words, *holos*, meaning "completely," and *kaustos*, meaning "burnt." Completely burnt. And the Jews surely would have been, had the world not gone to war.

10. Wiesel, *Night*, 34.

11. Pope Benedict XVI, quoted in Richard Cohen, "Whose Silence?" *www.washingtonpost.com/wp-dyn/content/article/2006/06/05/AR2006060501284.html* (accessed November 2, 2007).

12. Job 29:4.

13. John 11:35.

14. 1 Thessalonians 4:13.

15. Luke 7:13.

16. Matthew 4:16.

17. Hosea 2:19.

18. Luke 13:34.

19. Job 42:7.

20. Luke 12:4 – 5.

21. John 16:33.

22. See Job 38 – 41.

23. Madeleine L'Engle, *Two-Part Invention: The Story of a Marriage* (New York: HarperCollins, 1988), 152.

24. Madeleine L'Engle, *Walking on Water* (Colorado Springs: Shaw Books, 1980), 48.

25. Ibid., 134 – 35.

26. Madeleine L'Engle, *A Circle of Quiet* (New York: HarperCollins, 1972), 174.

27. "Letter: Remembering Everyone Who Died in the VT Tragedy," *www.the33rdstone.com* (accessed November 2, 2007).

Part 2
Echoes of Eden:
Remembering the World That Was

1. Psalm 69:34.

2. Psalm 46:10.

3. The story of my journey through and out of depression is told in *Losing God: Clinging to Faith through Doubt and Depression* (Downers Grove: InterVarsity, 2008).

4. Genesis 1:31.

5. Michael Card, *Scribbling in the Sand* (Downers Grove: InterVarsity, 2002), 32.

6. "This Is My Father's World," Maltbie Davenport Babcock, 1901. Public domain.

7. Ibid.

8. Ibid.

9. "Heritage Project Celebrates Five Years of Harvesting the Best Images from Hubble Space Telescope," *http://hubblesite.org/newscenter/archive/releases/2003/28/image/a* (accessed November 10, 2007).

10. Ibid.

11. *http://en.wikipedia.org/wiki/The_Universe* (accessed November 10, 2007).

12. "This Is My Father's World."

13. Romans 1:20.

14. Isaiah 6:3.

15. Psalm 19:1, emphasis added.

16. Ecclesiastes 3:1, 4 KJV.

17. Madeleine L'Engle, *Two-Part Invention: The Story of a Marriage* (New York: HarperCollins, 1988), 169.

18. Philippians 4:8.

19. Philippians 4:8 NLT.

20. Chris Tomlin, "How Great Is Our God" (Brentwood, Tenn.: Sparrow Records, 2004).

21. 1 John 2:8; Romans 13:12.

22. James 1:17.

23. Philip Yancey, "Where Is God When It Hurts? A Sermon Given on the Virginia Tech Campus Two Weeks after the Shootings," *Christianity Today*, June 2007, 56.

24. Hebrews 1:3.

25. Philip Yancey, *Reaching for the Invisible God* (Grand Rapids: Zondervan, 2000), 138–39.

26. Romans 5:6.

27. Philip Yancey, "Where Is God When It Hurts? A Sermon Given on the Virginia Tech Campus Two Weeks after the Shootings," *Christianity Today*, June 2007, 58.

28. Philip Yancey, *Reaching for the Invisible God* (Grand Rapids: Zondervan, 2000), 224.

29. 1 Corinthians 4:7 NLT.

30. John 1:5 NASB.

31. Josh Keller, "Profiles of the Slain: Victims in the Virginia Tech Shootings," posted April 19, 2007, *Chronicle of Higher Education*: *http://chronicle.com/news/ profiles/2085/matthew-la-porte* (accessed November 23, 2007).

32. Corinthian Kelly, quoted in Neil Harvey, "Matthew La Porte: 'Troubled Boy' Grew into a Corps Leader," posted April 17, 2007, *Roanoke Times*: *www.roanoke.com/vtvictims/wb/113509* (accessed November 23, 2007).

33. Harvey, "Matthew La Porte."

34. Kevin Kocur, quoted in "Massacre at Virginia Tech: In Their Honor." *CNN.com*: *www.cnn.com/SPECIALS/2007/virginiatech.shootings/victims/ profiles/matthew.laporte.html* (accessed November 23, 2007).

35. "Times Topics: Matt La Porte," *New York Times*: *http://topics.nytimes. com/top/reference/timestopics/people/l/matt_la_porte/index.html* (accessed November 23, 2007).

36. Ibid.

37. Lt. Col. Rodney P. Grove, quoted in "Times Topics: Matt La Porte."

38. "New Images: Red Rocks and Dinosaur Ridge," *Earth Observatory*: *http://earthobservatory.nasa.gov/Newsroom/NewImages/images.php3?img_ id=17126* (accessed November 24, 2007).

39. Madeleine L'Engle, *Two-Part Invention: The Story of a Marriage* (New York: HarperCollins, 1988), 169.

40. Matthew 14:13.

41. Richard J. Foster, *Celebration of Discipline: The Path to Spiritual Growth* (New York: HarperCollins, 1978), 97.

42. Ibid., 98.

43. Annie Dillard, *Pilgrim at Tinker Creek* (New York: HarperCollins, 1974), 230.

44. Ecclesiastes 1:11.

45. Job 14:14.

46. "Earthquake Rocks Japan: Powerful Quake Kills 5, Injures over 500," *Fox News*: *www.foxnews.com/photoessay/0,4644,2053,00.html* (accessed November 25, 2007).

47. "Earthquake Rocks Northern Japan," *BBC News*: *http://news.bbc.co.uk/2/ hi/asia-pacific/4155026.stm* (accessed November 25, 2007).

48. Ibid.

49. Annie Dillard, *Pilgrim at Tinker Creek* (New York: HarperCollins, 1974), 270.

50. Annie Dillard, *For the Time Being* (New York: Vintage Books, 1999), 109.

51. "Tsunami Death Toll Passes 283,000," *www.smh.com.au/news/Asia-Tsunami/Tsunami-death-toll-passes−283000/2005/01/27/1106415737181.html* (accessed November 10, 2007).

52. "2004 Indian Ocean Earthquake," *http://en.wikipedia.org/wiki/2004_Indian_Ocean_earthquake* (accessed November 10, 2007).

53. Exodus 14:21−22.

54. Exodus 14:27.

55. Romans 8:20−22 NLT.

56. Dillard, *Pilgrim at Tinker Creek*, 232, 237.

Part 3
Breathless Expectation:
Imagining the World That Will Be

1. Sammy Cahn and Jule Styne, "Let It Snow, Let It Snow, Let It Snow" (Beverly Hills: Cahn Music Company, 1945).

2. Revelation 11:15.

3. Matthew 6:10.

4. "This Is My Father's World," Maltbie Davenport Babcock, 1901. Public domain.

5. Colossians 3:2 NLT (1997).

6. Philippians 3:20.

7. 1 Peter 1:13 NIV.

8. Romans 8:23, emphasis added.

9. 1 Corinthians 1:7, emphasis added.

10. Galatians 5:5, emphasis added.

11. Philippians 3:20, emphasis added.

12. 2 Timothy 4:8, emphasis added.

13. Revelation 21:1−5.

14. Oswald Chambers, *My Utmost for His Highest* (Grand Rapids: Discovery House, 1935), 86 (April 29 entry).

15. I have in mind Romans 8:21, where Paul says creation will be "liberated," and 2 Peter 3:10−13, where Peter says "everything will be destroyed."

16. 1 Corinthians 2:9 NIV.

17. Matthew 18:3.

18. Matthew 19:14.

19. Luke 18:27.

20. Mark 10:27.

21. Matthew 5:4.

22. Luke 6:21.

23. See Jesus' prayer in John 17.

24. Graham Tomlin, *The Provocative Church* (London: SCPK, 2002), 22.

25. Madeleine L'Engle, *A Circle of Quiet* (New York: HarperCollins, 1972), 99.

26. C. S. Lewis, *A Grief Observed* (New York: HarperCollins, 1961), 27–28.

27. Romans 6:23.

28. 1 Corinthians 15:16–18.

29. 1 Corinthians 15:20–23.

30. "Decomposition," *http://en.wikipedia.org/wiki/Decomposition* (accessed January 9, 2008).

31. "Putrefaction," *http://en.wikipedia.org/wiki/Putrefaction* (accessed January 9, 2008).

32. Annie Dillard, *For the Time Being* (New York: Vintage Books, 1999), 118.

33. "Cremation," *http://en.wikipedia.org/wiki/Cremation* (accessed January 9, 2008).

34. Habakkuk 1:2.

35. 2 Peter 3:9.

36. Philip Yancey, "Where Is God When It Hurts? A Sermon Given on the Virginia Tech Campus Two Weeks after the Shootings," *Christianity Today*, June, 2007, 59.

37. Matthew 10:42.

38. 2 Corinthians 8:9.

39. N. T. Wright.

40. 1 Thessalonians 5:15 NIV

41. Luke 6:35.

42. 2 Corinthians 11:24–28.

43. 2 Corinthians 1:8.

44. Philippians 4:4.

45. 2 Corinthians 6:10.

46. 2 Corinthians 5:8.

47. Philippians 1:23.

48. Shauna Niequist, *Cold Tangerines* (Grand Rapids: Zondervan, 2007), 231.

49. Thornton Wilder, *Our Town* (New York: Coward-McCann, 1938), 81.

50. Ibid., 82.

51. Ibid., 83.

52. Ibid.

53. Ibid.

54. Ibid.

55. Paul uses this term frequently throughout his letters, referring not to a special group of believers but to all believers in Christ.

56. 1 Corinthians 10:31.

57. C. S. Lewis, *The Problem of Pain* (New York: Touchstone, 1940), 103.

58. Proverbs 14:10.

59. Larry Hincker, "Statement by President Charles W. Steger in Response to Virginia Tech Review Panel Report," posted August 30, 2007, *www.vtnews. vt.edu/story.php?relyear=2007&itemno=490* (accessed December 9, 2007).

60. 1 Corinthians 12:26.

61. Luke 13:2–5.

62. John 14:6.

63. Psalm 13:3.

64. "The First Noel," traditional English carol. Public domain.

65. 1 John 2:8.

66. John Piper, *God Is the Gospel* (Wheaton, Ill.: Crossway, 2005).

67. Job 42:3.

68. Luke 2:25.

69. Luke 2:26.

70. Luke 2:29–32.

71. After writing the book, I learned from Chris Hutto that Matt La Porte was on scholarship with the air force and planning on a career as an intelligence officer. "This suited his personality perfectly," Chris says.

72. Romans 8:18.

73. Revelation 22:20.

74. Annie Dillard, *The Writing Life* (New York: HarperPerennial, 1990), 79.

"If God forgets you, it is as though you have never
existed. . . . You are a tale told by an idiot;
forgotten; annihilated."
—Madeleine L'Engle

LOSING GOD
Clinging to Faith Through Doubt and Depression
Matt Rogers

Coming November 2008

Share Your Thoughts

With the Author: Your comments will be forwarded to the author when you send them to *zauthor@zondervan.com*.

With Zondervan: Submit your review of this book by writing to *zreview@zondervan.com*.

Free Online Resources at
www.zondervan.com/hello

 Zondervan AuthorTracker: Be notified whenever your favorite authors publish new books, go on tour, or post an update about what's happening in their lives.

 Daily Bible Verses and Devotions: Enrich your life with daily Bible verses or devotions that help you start every morning focused on God.

 Free Email Publications: Sign up for newsletters on fiction, Christian living, church ministry, parenting, and more.

 Zondervan Bible Search: Find and compare Bible passages in a variety of translations at www.zondervanbiblesearch.com.

 Other Benefits: Register yourself to receive online benefits like coupons and special offers, or to participate in research.